NOT THAT WHEEL, JESUS!

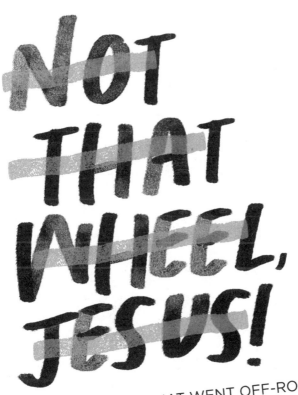

NOT ~~THAT~~ ~~WHEEL,~~ ~~JESUS!~~

STORIES FROM A FAITH THAT WENT OFF-ROAD IN THE BEST (AND WORST) POSSIBLE WAYS

MARY ~~KATHERINE~~ BACKSTROM

WORTHY
PUBLISHING
New York • Nashville

Disclaimer: Let's be honest—I have a dramatic brain and enough trauma to make my memory Swiss cheese, so I've been left to piece together the rest, and I've done the best I can. This is my story, as I remember it. If you remember it differently, write a book. I really would love to read that.

Some names have been changed, and some individuals are composites. If some of my people remind you of yourself…congrats, my friend! Or, my apologies. I guess that depends entirely on your life choices.

Worthy
Hachette Book Group
1290 Avenue of the Americas, New York, NY 10104
worthypublishing.com
@WorthyPub

First Edition: August 2025

Worthy is a division of Hachette Book Group, Inc. The Worthy name and logo are registered trademarks of Hachette Book Group, Inc.

The publisher is not responsible for websites (or their content) that are not owned by the publisher.

The Hachette Speakers Bureau provides a wide range of authors for speaking events. To find out more, go to hachettespeakersbureau.com or email HachetteSpeakers@hbgusa.com.

Scripture quotations marked (NIV) are taken from the Holy Bible, New International Version®. Copyright © 1973, 1978,1984, 2011 by Biblica, Inc.™ Used by permission of Zondervan. All rights reserved worldwide. www.zondervan.com. The "NIV" and "New International Version" are trademarks registered in the United States Patent and Trademark Office by Biblica, Inc.™ Scripture quotations marked KJV are from the King James Version of the Holy Bible. In the public domain.

Worthy Books may be purchased in bulk for business, educational, or promotional use. For information, please contact your local bookseller or the Hachette Book Group Special Markets Department at special.markets@hbgusa.com.

Library of Congress Cataloging-in-Publication Data

Names: Backstrom, Mary Katherine author
Title: Not that wheel, Jesus! : stories from a faith that went off-road in the best (and worst) possible ways / Mary Katherine Backstrom.
Description: First edition. | Nashville : Worthy Books, 2025.
Identifiers: LCCN 2025009452 | ISBN 9781546004189 hardcover | ISBN 9781546004202 ebook
Subjects: LCSH: Backstrom, Mary Katherine | Christian biography—United States | Christian women—Religious life | LCGFT: Autobiographies
Classification: LCC BR1725.B28 A3 2025 | DDC 277.308/3092 $a B—dc23/eng/20250506
LC record available at https://lccn.loc.gov/2025009452

ISBNs: 9781546004189 (hardcover), 9781546004202 (ebook)

Printed in the United States of America

LSC-H

Printing 1, 2025

To Caroline, Cole, Cooper, and Cate—for opening your hearts and letting me into your world.

I love it here. And I love you BIG.

CONTENTS

NOT THAT WHEEL, JESUS!

CHAPTER 1

Jesus, Take the Wheel

For the first thirty-two years of my life, I self-identified as the Weirdest Person in All the Rooms. From childhood to college, and even in the bonds of marriage, this was the throne that I claimed. My personality is that of the comic relief, the one who breaks the ice with a sledgehammer. My stories were the strangest, my laugh the most unhinged, my jokes the most off-the-wall.

And then, I met Sara Baker.

It's not often that you'll find a queen who is happy to lose her throne, but I was happy to lose this one. In exchange for losing the title of the Weirdest Person in All the Rooms, I gained the funniest, most wonderful damn friend in the world.

For every ridiculous story I have, she has one that is a bit more ridiculous. For every witty punch line I land, she has some cheese to melt on top. And it's not that she's a one-upper. That's not Sara's style. That woman does not hold back, but she also competes with no one. I know she's always ready to provide the assist. It's just who she is, from the outside in, from her flawless skin to her funny bones.

You might be picking up on the fact that I love this woman, and that's true. Sara's my bestie. She's one-third of the trio that make up my Wolfpack, with Meredith completing the trinity. Mer is the glue that pieces us back together when we fall apart and the voice of reason that tugs us back down to earth. Sara's the third that makes us laugh 'til we cry, or cry 'til we laugh.

One Monday, I'd just dropped my kids off at school after a particularly rough morning at home. I needed a friend, and since my besties are in two opposite time zones, there's always someone up when I need an ear. Since Mer was still snoring in Utah, I called the one who wouldn't kill me. It was 9:00 a.m. in Maryland when Sara picked up.

I was about to unpack the specifics of my failings to Sara as I was driving home from drop-off: how my daughter's hair was still unbrushed, how my son ate a cookie for breakfast, how I'd managed to leave the house without a bra. But just as I was opening my mouth, a cat darted in front of my car. I swerved hard to the left, my tires screeching in protest. A horn blasted from the car just behind me. And as that stupid feline scampered back to safety in a bush by the road, I screamed:

"What the hell, Joe?!"

For a moment, there was silence at the end of the line. Then

Sara expressed love the only way she knows how—panicked concern peppered with a string of colorful expletives.

"MK! *bleepity bleeeep.* What *bleepity bleep* just happened?! Are you alive?"

Just barely.

"I...I just about died for a cat."

"Well, that's a dumbass way to die." There's my girl. "Wait. Who the hell is Joe?"

I couldn't help but laugh. I didn't even remember saying it.

I explained that years ago, my stepdad was driving the family to dinner. I was in the backseat of this old Jeep, and the top was off. It was your typical, beautiful country drive. Zac Brown on the radio, wind in our hair, the whole deal.

Until a squirrel ran out directly in front of the Jeep. And Joe didn't really swerve so much as launch us forward against our seat belts before throwing us back into our seats. It's like he hesitated for a microsecond and thought about it...and then ran over the damn thing.

Thump.

Maybe I was hormonal, or maybe I was unmedicated, but I believed he'd swerved on purpose—not to avoid the squirrel—but to run it over.

So, I screamed.

"WHAT THE HELL, JOE?!"

And God bless the man, he was absolutely mortified. He felt so terrible. And it's funny now, because he's the most gentle man in the world, and while he was clearly trying to avoid a catastrophe with a carful of precious cargo, I interpreted his choice as intentional squirrel slaughter. And in the way that weird, gruesome things can become funny over time, so it happened with the Jeep and Joe and the flattened squirrel. It became a family joke. Anytime a creature runs out in the road, our family yells,

"WHAT THE HELL, JOE?!"

Another pause on Sara's end. "If those had been your last words—"

"You'd put them on my gravestone."

"Absolutely."

"I'd expect nothing less. But can we talk about the fact that I just about died for some feral fleabag?"

"Again—the absolute dumbest way to die. Have I ever told you about the time I got cut out of a wreck with the Jaws of Life because I swerved to avoid a cat?"

You know how I said Sara always has a story? Well, this one was no exception. She was twenty years old, driving home from work on a South Carolina highway when an orange cat darted across the road, and, like me, she swerved hard to the left. Unlike me, though, Sara lost control of her car and went flying into a tree-filled median. Her car was crushed like a tuna can, and they had to cut her out of the wreckage. Luckily, she emerged (mostly) unscathed, with little more than a scrape to her finger. I like to imagine that orange cat gifted Sara one of its multiple lives, because based on a picture of that little car's wreckage, she shouldn't have survived it at all.

I wanted to laugh, and we did for a minute. But then the absurdity of the whole thing hit me.

One of my very favorite people, one of the brightest lights in my world, was almost extinguished. And for what?

I mean, don't get me wrong, I love furry critters. I currently have six too many. But I think we should all agree that a human soul weighs a little bit more.

And yet, without a single thought for our own mortality, Sara and I made the same dumb decision. To preserve the existence of whatever was ahead by driving ourselves off the road.

No matter the potential consequences, or the cost to our own precious lives, when it came down to that split-second steering wheel decision…

We just couldn't kill the damn cats.

. . . .

A few years ago, I was driving my son home from church and noticed my notorious chatterbox was being rather quiet. Typically with Ben, I struggled to get a word in edgewise. Radio silence from the backseat? My Spidey senses were activated.

"Hey, kiddo." I turned the radio down. "Whatcha thinkin' about? Everything okay?"

I watched his face in the rearview mirror and frowned at the tears I saw gathering.

"Momma, do you believe that when GG dies, she's gonna go to hell?"

My stomach hollowed out. I felt a pang of nausea.

What made him ask such a thing?

Ben and GG were both five years old and had been best friends since they were in Pampers. They held hands walking into their first day of preschool. They were teammates on their first soccer team (the Purple Sharks had a losing season, but GG and Ben were only in it for the Capri Suns, anyway). And now, he was sitting in his car seat, worried. Not only about his best friend dying—but that she might burn. Forever.

Until that very moment of life—I mean that actual, precise moment—I had an answer to this question. If somebody dies, and they don't believe in Jesus, they go straight to hell.

Black-and-white.

Simple.

GG had never been taught about Jesus, aside from the cultural context that everyone learns at Christmas. She certainly didn't believe in Jesus and would likely never convert. Her parents—my best friends—are the best people that I've ever known. Both caring physicians, generous citizens, and loyal and supportive friends. They are good people—down to their core. But GG's mother is nonreligious and her father is Jewish, and neither are particularly evangelical. So, if I was going by the book—or rather, what I'd been told about said book—none of their goodness would matter at all.

They were unsaved and therefore condemned.

But when I looked into those teary green eyes and saw the fear in my little boy's heart, I was faced with the enormity and weight of that answer.

And suddenly, I didn't know.

I didn't know what to say. I didn't know what to do. What I had just moments before been unwaveringly sure of no longer seemed right. How could it be? It hit me right in the chest, how inappropriate it was for something so infinite to be so black-and-white. It certainly wasn't simple.

So, I did something that felt equal parts unnatural and necessary. I asked his opinion. And even as the words exited my mouth, I felt I was flirting with damnation.

"Baby, people believe so many different things. I want to know what you think."

He blinked, and his tiny fist rubbed away a tear. Glancing back, I could see his thoughts churning.

"I think...that if God loves everybody...then He wouldn't hurt GG like that."

And as Ben's tiny voice trembled with both hope and uncertainty—I felt something tear in my heart. A thread tugging loose from a carefully knit sweater I'd been wearing my whole entire life.

It reminds me of that Weezer song.

Tell me you know about Weezer.

To be fair, I probably shouldn't have had that album when I was in middle school, but like so many millennial kids, I grew up sharing a bedroom with an older sister.

Karen Leigh is five years older than me, and if there was a poster child for that Duck Head shorts–wearing, grunge rock–listening generation, she'd be it. From Nirvana to the Off-spring, from Beastie Boys to Green Day. I received quite the real-world education from the music she blasted out of her boom box. But I always got excited when she opened up her CD orga-nizer and selected a particular bright teal album with the musical stylings of a little group known as…Weezer.

Weezer spoke to my puberty-ravaged soul. It was just the right mixture of moody and mad, and if some of you are judging me right now, I accept that. It wasn't until recently that I dis-covered that Weezer is a very polarizing band in that Nickelback kinda way.

But to be honest, I loved them, and I still kinda do. "Buddy Holly" and "Say It Ain't So" are two of my go-to karaoke selec-tions. But my all-time favorite Weezer song is "Undone." Every sin-gle time that hazy guitar riff begins, and the band starts chattering back and forth, I am drawn in like a little grunge moth to a flame.

"The Sweater Song" (as "Undone" was also called) became an anthem for weirdos like me. We didn't need to know what it was about. To be honest, I'm still not sure if it's a commentary on sex or depression or just a series of dumb lyrics. I have no idea if it's meant to be taken seriously or with a heavy dose of irony. But it spoke to my little sixth-grade heart. There was just something about those lyrics that got to the young twelve-year-old me.

"If you want to destroy my sweater, hold this thread as I walk away."

And in that car, after Ben asked that question, I knew I had no choice but to pull that thread.

It was my undoing, his tiny voice asking me about hell. It was the very first rip in the fabric of a series of threads I'd been holding together my whole life. It wasn't that I'd never answered a question like his before. I had, plenty of times, to people who asked it in a variety of settings and for a variety of reasons. As a youth group leader, an overseas missionary to Thailand, when I worked in college campus ministry. For practically my entire life, I had the answer to this question. But when my son asked, the words I'd spit out so casually before, practiced and prepped for a Christianese response—well, this time, those words didn't come.

More than that, they couldn't come. A visceral part of me balked. It was the same instinct that swats tiny hands from the stove. The same instinct that would cause a parent to run over an animal instead of risking the children in the backseat.

It was electric in my veins. As if answering his question would place him in front of that car.

Of course, a small child wouldn't be sent to hell…right?

What on earth was my problem?

For the rest of that night, I felt like I might be losing my mind. The unease nagged at me well past the time when I should have been asleep. And the more I thought about it, the further I felt from what I thought I knew. I could feel myself walking away from something.

But that something couldn't be God.

Could it?

That question sent a shiver through my body.

No. That couldn't be it.

I believed, with my whole heart, that God was real. And not only that, but that God was good. I never needed Scripture to convince me of that truth. I'd seen the evidence scattered throughout the whole world. When I listened to the ocean break over the rocky cliffs of Ogunquit, Maine, that roar was the sound of my God. When I hiked the quiet forests of Monte Sano Mountain, His peace swelled like a river inside me. When I stepped onto my back porch in the middle of an Alabama summer, there He was, in the constant thrum of the cicada songs and the quiet blink-blinks of the lightning bugs.

Whenever I connected with the beauty of creation, my heart couldn't help but sing. It was a song, both ancient and deeply familiar. One that whispered: Creator. As if those trees and the ocean and even my very bones all communed over some long-held secret.

No. That's not something I could leave if I tried. The essence of my faith—my belief in God—remained. And still, I felt myself walking.

If you want to destroy my sweater, hold this thread as I walk away...

I didn't know it then, but at that moment, driving my son home from church, a new season of life was beginning. An unraveling that I couldn't prevent and had no ability to stop. A season of questions that had no answers. A season that would cut me to the quick and also bring healing and personal growth.

And I wasn't gonna stop until I'd destroyed that sweater and saw the whole naked truth for myself.

I'd be lying if I told you it didn't feel strange to have what had always felt like rock-solid aspects of my faith suddenly punctuated with question marks. To be honest, "strange" would be the understatement of the century. I wasn't just some fly-by-night Easter Sunday sorta Christian. I had a bona fide evangelical pedigree. Raised as a Baptist in the Bible Belt South, I went to church every Sunday and Wednesday—even Fridays during church basketball season. (The TBC girls were the Christian league champs, though the Methodists gave us a run for our money.)

I was a youth group leader, played guitar in the worship band, and eventually even served as a missionary. All that to say, I knew my way around Scripture. I knew how our church interpreted Scripture, and more than that, I defended those doctrines.

I was sincerely passionate about my beliefs, but the thing is…I was also a child. My entire theology, start to finish, came straight from the mouth of my pastor. I received and believed and never dare questioned. Or at least, I'd stopped asking the questions out loud. But the contradictions had always been there, lingering in the back of my mind.

Like, how did polar bears and lizards all survive in one climate after getting off the ark?

Was God surprised by the sin of humankind? Shouldn't He have seen that one coming?

Why did God place a bet with Satan and then ruin Job's life just to win it?

For years, I've swerved around challenging faith questions the same way I've swerved around road critters. I was more than willing to crash into a ditch if it meant protecting the status quo.

Does my church harm people? Swerve.

Does God love gay people? Swerve.

Will my nonbelieving friends really go to hell?

HARD SWERVE.

Until kids. Until the practiced answers I knew by heart didn't feel so true anymore. Let me tell you, the journey of faith feels a whole lot different when your babies are in the car.

The last couple of years, ever since Ben asked that question, I've been in a faith crisis that required its own Jaws of Life. And I can't help but think it was one swerve too many that landed me in that ditch. Airbag exploded, glass on the floorboard, questioning all my life choices. Jesus glaring from the passenger side, still clinging to the Oh Shit handle.

It's a scary thing to reach the middle of your life and not know for sure what you believe. I mean, I knew what I'd been taught, and I knew what I'd accepted, but I'd never allowed myself to be curious. To allow space for the doubts and the bedtime questions that surely God isn't afraid of. I needed to find answers—not just for Ben, but most importantly, for myself.

But just like sweet Joe chose to hear the thump of something furry and precious under his wheel to keep all of us intact, I had to change my steering strategy. I had to stop skirting those pop-up questions and learn to just…keep moving toward them.

• • • • • • • • •

When I was in college there was this cheesy pop country song that dominated the airwaves. You know, the one that was sung by Carrie Underwood right after she won *American Idol*?

Yep, that one: "Jesus, Take the Wheel."

To be honest, I pretty much hated that song. The lyrics just about drove me crazy. Because what kind of mom lets go of the wheel while she's sliding on a sheet of black ice? Ma'am, there's a whole entire child in your car. Could you be a bit more proactive?

But also, I get it.

Or at least, I was starting to. My faith was spinning out in real time, and I was losing the illusion of control. I wasn't in charge of where this was going, or the questions that kept bringing more questions. I was very much in a spiritual tailspin, holding on for dear life.

It was dizzying, losing sight of the lines that had kept me on the straight and narrow. I needed to get this thing back on the road, but how?

I felt very much like a drunk driver must feel. So, in an act of broken desperation, I relinquished control of the drive. With the black ice beneath me and the tires screeching loudly, I prayed a prayer that surprised even me, the control-freak, know-everything, bona fide Baptist: "Jesus, take the wheel."

CHAPTER 2

Bedtime Questions

The first time I was baptized, I was just a little baby. Held up by my parents in the front of a Central Presbyterian Church like Simba in a frilly, smocked gown. I was committed to God, sprinkled with water, and, for a decade or so, that was that. But as I got older, my sins got sinnier, and it was determined I needed more water.

The second time I was baptized, I was fourteen. It was sometime around Halloween, and a classmate invited me to *Heaven's Gates & Hell's Flames*, which was being pitched as the Christian alternative to our local haunted houses. In the '90s, evangelical Christians sorted everything on the planet into one of two categories: "secular" or "Christian." Church kids didn't listen to secular bands; we listened to DC Talk. Youth groups didn't read Harry Potter (secular magic); we had *The Chronicles of Narnia* (Christian magic!). My secular peers screamed themselves hoarse when zombies and creepy clowns popped up around them on horror-themed Halloween hayrides. And my fellow Jesus Freaks and I had Hell Houses.

We rebranded everything in the name of our Lord and Savior, even actual brands. My favorite T-shirt looked just like a Sprite can, but instead of the traditional logo, it read "Spirit." When I say I was the Most Basic of All Youth Group Kids, I mean pH level 14. All that to say, while a holy haunted house would probably not appeal to most reasonable people, to the 1996 me, it sounded downright delightful. So I bought tickets and invited all my friends, and it was exactly as bizarre as you'd probably expect it to be.

The Hell House (as it was nicknamed) was divided into multiple rooms, where actors introduced us to three separate storylines. There was a family in the car driving home from vacation, a girl getting ready for her very first date, and a boy who was hanging out with friends. The scenes were short, but dripping with red flags. Any youth group kid worth their weight in salt would know there was danger ahead.

First of all, Car Dad was fighting with his wife because she wanted him to go to church. The kids were crying in the backseat and the scene ended with Car Dad yelling that he wasn't going, because "GOD IS NOT REAL!"

So, I knew he was definitely going to die.

And that teenage girl getting ready for the date? She was putting on too much makeup. And in case we weren't picking up the hints they were laying down, the scene ended with her calling a friend to say, "I'm going all the way tonight!" So, she was either gonna get pregnant or die, or both. If I had to guess, probably the latter. Loving a good two-for-one is universal.

And then there was Party Boy, who was totally done for because he'd already opened a beer.

The crowd was ushered into the next room, which was utterly dark and quiet. The air was warm and I noticed an unsettling smell. Something like burning plastic. Then, a speaker crackled to life, playing a recorded series of phone calls.

Party Boy was already drunk (called it) and on his way to pick up his date. Who was, you guessed it, Too-Much-Makeup Girl. The connections were making themselves as obvious as the final act in an episode of *This Is Us*. Based on the ominous music thumping out of the speakers, I deduced the young couple wouldn't be making it far, much less all the way that night. Car Dad and his family were in another vehicle, everyone still arguing, and then—*CRASH!* A loud explosion shook the room.

I gotta hand it to Calvary Baptist Church; I really underestimated just how hellacious their little Hell House would be. When the lights flickered on, in the center of the room was a wreckage of actual cars. Actors were on the floor, screaming in agony, covered in costume carnage. It was a disturbing sight, but before we could fully process everything, we were ushered into another room.

The brightly lit room was trimmed with gold paper and decorated with white fluffy clouds. On a stage was an intricate throne, where an enormous robed man sat. He looked like King Triton but carried a Bible. To his left stood multiple angels, and to his right…a younger, more attractive bearded man wearing Chacos, who, I had to assume, was Jesus.

So, we were in the throne room of God. Which means things were about to get interesting. Next thing I knew, a group of angels burst through a cloud-covered door, escorting the family of four. Apparently, everyone had died.

"Welcome, Elizabeth! Welcome, Paul! Welcome, Maggie and Scott!" the voice of the Triton God boomed, and I wondered for a moment if he was the guy who announced all our football games. The dead family shuffled up to the foot of the throne, where Dad was now shaking in terror. He'd just realized God was real.

"WAIT!" the dad yelped. "I'm not ready to die! I have a big meeting on Tuesday!"

God looked annoyed, and that made me giggle. An escort angel cut me a look.

"Paul Smith," His voice again boomed. "Do you know My Son, Jesus Christ?"

The man frantically looked to his wife and then his children, as if hoping for a bit of support.

"Yes! Please! I love Your Son!" Dad turned toward the Chaco Jesus. "Jesus, please! Tell Him I love You!"

Jesus shrugged, as if saying, "Sorry, bro, I can't help you now." And that's when the real panic set in. Paul threw himself down at the feet of God, begging for one more chance. And God, seemingly unbothered by this spectacle, gestured at a nearby angel.

"The Book of Life!" He demanded, and the angel handed it over. God opened up the tome straight to the middle, where I suppose all the Smiths could be found. He dragged a huge finger down the page for a moment before shaking His head in disappointment.

"Paul Smith, your name is not written in this book. Depart from me! I NEVER KNEW YOU!"

Suddenly, from the other side of the room, another hidden door burst open. And this time, some terrible-looking demons came barging into the room. Cackling and dancing, they grabbed poor Paul and dragged him away from the throne. His children were screaming, "NO! NO! NOT DADDY!" But a moment later, he was gone. The door slammed shut, and the vibe in the room got weird. I couldn't help but think this wasn't the most compassionate way to do things, and if I were God...

"Elizabeth Smith. Maggie Smith. Scott Smith. Come." My thoughts were interrupted by Triton God coaxing the rest of the family forward.

"Do you know My Son, Jesus Christ? Are your names in My Book of Life?"

Chaco Jesus smiled and took a small step forward. "Lord, I know them well."

And at this news, the family squealed with delight and ran straight into His arms. Then, an angel pointed them toward a golden door, where they were escorted straight into heaven. They hugged Jesus and celebrated all the way out the door. And I'm sure they were genuinely delighted. But I have to admit I was a little weirded out by how quickly they forgot poor old Dad.

I didn't have time to ponder those details too long, because the door from earth was flung open once more, and in stumbled two very confused teenagers. Party Boy was still holding his beer, and God made quick work of them both. As the demons dragged the duo straight into hell, I muttered, "Well, that was a terrible date." A bunch of teenagers standing nearby decided it was the greatest thing they'd ever heard. I was not going for the greatest thing, I was going for a small giggle. But I guess that joke really got away from me because the next thing I knew, Triton God looked angry. At least two of the four escort angels were actively sneering at me.

I realized I'd taken things a bit too far, and if I didn't play my cards just right, some small-town momma was gonna make it her business to issue my momma a full report. The best thing I could do was go quiet for the evening. Draw as little attention as possible. But when God spoke next, my stomach fell straight to my butt.

"Hark! Hark! Judgment Day is near! Is your name in God's Book of Life?"

As the angel started reading names from the book, I suddenly felt my stomach leap back up as if one of those scary, secular-hayride clowns had jumped out in front of me. I remembered that the tickets for this Hell House had a form on the back meant for attendees to fill out. It was basic information, things like our name, age, address, and phone number, which I didn't mind sharing. But Momma did.

God bless her, she'd said, "If you give them your name, they're gonna start calling, and I don't wanna deal with all that." I figured she was right, so I used a fake name and so did my friends.

I'll be honest and admit that we had a very good time with that exercise. But when we wrote our fake names, I think we were expecting that they'd be read by some church secretary. Somebody who wore floral and ate peppermints all day, who would read them and toss them away.

What we sure didn't expect was an angel of God to read them straight from the Book of Life.

Oh no. Oh no. Oh. NO. NO. NO.

"Harry Butt? Ben Dover? Are your names in this Book of Life?"

My face went red. How had we not thought this scenario through? There is zero plausible deniability once you invite Harry Butt to the party. I was going to cry or laugh or maybe both. No way could this really be happening. My friends were frozen, eyes wide in horror. Each of us avoiding eye contact, lest we laugh and get dragged straight to hell by an escort who knew our mommas. I bit my tongue and tried not to explode.

"Anita Burger? Hugh Jazz? Are your names in this Book of Life?"

I saw the moment the angel realized. And that's when I knew we were done for. He slammed the Book of Life shut and pointed to the crowd, but it felt like he especially marked me.

"Repent of your sins or judgment will come! OUR GOD WILL NOT BE MOCKED!"

I was wondering if that was a part of the script, or a message specifically for me, but the music cut on, and our escorts appeared to usher us away from God's throne, which honestly eased my mind. King Triton was a total buzzkill.

I sighed with relief. Thank goodness. We were finally going home.

And that's when I smelled the burning meat and heard some familiar screams. It was Car Dad and Party Boy and Too-Much-Makeup Girl, all of them wailing in agony. The show wasn't over. It was just getting started.

They called it "Hell House" for a reason.

Walking out, the first thing I noticed was all of the water. Volunteers in green Calvary Baptist shirts passing out bottles of water and students huddled up with their friends, clothes soaking wet, towels draped around their shoulders. It felt very much like we'd been spat out of hell into a very sad, very strange pool party.

The outdoor pool set up on the grass had a line of students wrapped around it. Two youth pastors were busy dunking folks in tandem. It was an assembly line for salvation.

A volunteer approached me with a bottle of water.

"Do you know if your name is in the Book of Life?" she asked me with a casual smile, as if she were inquiring about the weather and not acting as a customs agent for heaven holding the stamp on my passport to the afterlife.

"I mean, I think so. I believe in Jesus and I think God loves me."

"Do you think or do you know?"

"Is it possible to really know for sure? I mean, how did you know you were saved?"

"Well, sweetie, when you are truly saved, you just…know it. Right. In. Here." She patted her heart three times to further illustrate the point.

I had my doubts that things were really that simple. I'd read Psalms and there were entire chapters written by men with doubt. They asked God why He'd hidden His face from them when they were hurting. Was she telling me those guys weren't saved?

She said I'd know. Right. In. Here.

"Well, I do want to be certain." I hesitated. "I was christened as a child. Do you think that counts?"

"Oh, sweetie." The lady in the green T-shirt just shook her head. "That wasn't nearly enough water."

. . . .

It took me awhile to realize why I couldn't answer Ben's question about the fate of his best friend. Why his tiny voice inquiring about hell had triggered those alarm bells inside me. For a time, I suspected it was the theology of hell that had so seriously snagged my little faith sweater: Is eternal torment real?

So, I tried sorting it out. I read books, pestered pastors, and studied the Scriptures about hell in both translated and original languages. But when I really dug in and started searching for absolutes, something interesting happened. The more questions I asked, the more questions appeared. I wanted answers, but instead, my questions were multiplying like bunnies.

If eternal torment is real, then what about babies and children? Is there some magical age that kids suddenly hit, an age when they become accountable for their sins?

"Happy birthday, kiddo. You're officially condemned! Here's your cake! You can light your candle with the eternal flames."

Different churches had different answers, and I was shocked by how much they varied. Turns out, there isn't a global consensus regarding the Christian age of accountability.

Is it five years old? Ten? Eighteen? Twenty-one? It doesn't seem fair that you can serve your country and go to hell before legally ordering a beer.

Before long, I found myself trapped in a game of theological whack-a-mole. And that's when I ran face-first into a really big problem: I didn't want to ask these questions. It's not that I didn't want the answers; I did. The truth is, I was scared. Worse than that, I was traumatized. Half my life, I'd been trying to nurture my soul under the perpetual threat of damnation.

My spirit was infected with fear. I was bone-deep terrified of asking questions.

I'd been taught not to question church leaders, because to do that was to question God, and we all knew where that led.

Whenever a new question came up, I could hear my childhood pastor, smacking his lips with disapproval in the way he always did when I was a child and asked hard questions that didn't have Sunday school answers. As if my curiosity and desire to understand things deeply was an immediate threat to the heavens. I asked why an omnipresent God sometimes sent the Holy Spirit out like a scout. I asked why the Song of Solomon was so explicit, since the couple wasn't married. I asked big questions for such a young kid, and my challenges were treated like heresy.

But I wasn't trying to challenge my faith. I was trying to explore it more deeply. When the grown-ups didn't have an answer to my question, though, they would turn it right back at me.

Who was I to question God?

One of my favorite things about children is the questions they ask every day. Sometimes they're hilarious, sometimes they're exhausting, and, frequently, they're impossible to answer. I recently read an interview with author Warren Berger, who said that children ask an average of forty thousand questions between the ages of two and five. When I saw that number, I'll admit I was shocked.

Because, frankly, forty thousand seems low to me. I'd put money on the fact that my kids asked a million before they stepped foot into kindergarten. And I'd bet even more money that the majority of those questions were asked when they were in bed and were supposed to be sleeping. It's a universal truth in the parenting world that kids are never more curious or wiggly or thirsty than when it's time for bed.

When my son was about two, I created a little note on my iPhone titled "bedtime questions." And over the last seven years, I've kept a record of the most absurdly hilarious questions my children have asked me when they were most definitely supposed to be sleeping.

"If God is on a throne, but He's also in my heart, how is that throne not clogging up my blood?"

"Do you think that when we pull on the grass, it's like pulling on the earth's hair?"

"Okay, so a metaphor is like...you smell like a fart?"

"Are raw foods still alive? Am I raw?"

"If I take the seeds off my hamburger bun, can I grow my own hamburger at home?"

"Did lizards' legs fall off and become snakes or did snakes get tired and grow legs?"

"Sometimes my brain feels like yogurt. When you get tired of thinking does your brain ever feel like yogurt?"

I have more, so many more, but that's a whole 'nother book worth of content. What I'm getting at is this: Kids ask a buttload of ridiculous questions, and sometimes they can be frustrating. I can't tell you how many times I have uttered, "I don't know; go ask your dad," or "No more talking; you're supposed to be sleeping."

And then, just like every other phase of parenting, the Question Phase comes to an end. The kids get less curious, or perhaps they just stop asking...and all of a sudden you find yourself missing those bedtime inquisitions.

Remember that author I was telling you about? He reiterated this point. "Right around age five or six, questioning drops off a cliff," Warren said. "Children go to school as question marks and leave school as periods."

When I read that, it felt like a gut punch. I could feel my heart sigh with sadness.

What is it about the process of growing up that robs us of this beautiful curiosity?

Sometimes, I like to imagine that God has His own divine version of an iPhone note that He laughs and scrolls through from time to time. It'd be full of all sorts of curious questions that I've been asking over the years.

"Does eternity get boring? Do I have to wear robes?"

"Are there talking animals in heaven? Is my dead dog mad at me?"

"Do different sins have a points value?"

"Will I be young me or old me in the afterlife, or do I get to choose?"

"What are You going to do about the truly terrible people like Mussolini or Hitler? Do they get the same verdict as, say, a back-slidden Baptist (asking for a friend…)?"

"If I don't have to wear robes, do I have to wear the outfit I die in? What if I die in hard pants?"

For any of my friends reading this, just know "Are you mad at me?" is a popular question in the rotation. I know you're not surprised that even God can't escape that one.

And…

"What if I ask You something and I don't like Your answer? What if it doesn't line up with the idea of You I've spent a whole life building? And what happens if that means that while I love You, I'm not sure I like You? Or is that even possible? If it's possible, is it okay? And by the way, that whole hell thing? Surely a loving God wouldn't have a father dragged out of the throne room by demons while his children are screaming his name…right? Is that really how this whole thing goes?"

All while I'm supposed to be going to sleep.

While the questions my kids have been asking may be fewer and farther between these days, here's what I'm starting to figure out: I can't and don't want to swerve away from the questions my kids (or myself, for that matter) have about a loving God. I've played dodge-the-squirrel for as long as I can remember with the tough theological questions.

I want everything I believe to fit neatly in a storage system that is perfectly organized, color-coordinated, and labeled, thank you very much.

No frayed hems over here, no sir.

That is, until my sweater unraveled.

It's not lost on me that the prayer shawl Jesus would have worn probably had threads sprouting from its edges. The fringe was called a tzitzit, and I'm telling you that not because I'm fancy but because I can look things up on Wikipedia. Why let all kinds of threads hang down from a piece of fabric that embodied religion? There are all kinds of scholarly theories, but what I like to think is this: The edges of faith are supposed to be frayed.

Imperfect. Unfinished. Messy.

When we're honest, those threads are the places we pick up again and again, rolling those questions between our fingers, in an exercise that is half prayer and half plea.

For so long, I was taught that God was frustrated or even angry with my childlike curiosity, as if He were a deadbeat, emotionally unavailable dad with a terrible temper. As if bedtime questions were an act of spiritual defiance, and not a heartfelt attempt to connect more deeply with my Father.

There will always be people in positions of spiritual leadership who disagree with this notion—but I, for one, simply cannot believe that God is annoyed with my questions. Perhaps it's the way we've been taught to see God—as unyielding and literal as His words—that makes questioning feel like rebellion. But I believe that no kindhearted father would shame or condemn the honest curiosity of his own child.

Who are we to question God?

We're His wide-eyed, inquisitive children.

In the early years of marriage, when my husband was still in medical school, we relocated to Huntsville, Alabama, for the clinical portion of his training. There's a little area in town called the Medical District, just a few blocks away from the hospital, that used to be full of quaint little cottages with affordable rent for families. That's definitely not the case anymore, but it was in 2011.

I adored our time in that sunshine-yellow bungalow on Princeton Avenue. In the evenings I could hear the high school marching band practicing for the half-time show. And in the mornings, I would grab a cup of coffee, back out of my driveway for work, and look down the end of our quiet street toward the best dang view in the city.

No, not the rocket or Monte Sano Mountain.

I'm talking about Eggbeater Jesus.

One of the quirkiest landmarks in my childhood hometown is the mosaic at First Baptist Church, which local residents affectionately refer to as "the Eggbeater Jesus." The figure of Christ is 43 feet high and covers the front of the church. The mosaic was created with 1.4 million pieces of tile—each one as small as a thumbnail and painstakingly cut and hand-painted by artisans in Italy. Then, the tiles were shipped to Huntsville and carefully applied by the artist, Mr. Gordon Smith, using his fingers or tweezers.

It is one of the largest mosaics in the entire United States, but that's not why everyone loves it. Officially known as the Cosmic Christ, this ultramodern, colorful mosaic depicts Jesus floating among the cosmos, holding a star in His hands. It gives Age of Aquarius vibes to the front of a Baptist church. The whole thing is weird, considering the context. But believe it or not, it gets weirder.

In an artistic decision that will forever be lauded, Mr. Smith added lines to the bottom of Jesus' robe to represent centrifugal motion. One might even say he was trying to put a "spin" on Jesus (sorry, I had to).

Anyways, he succeeded, but with the unintended effect of turning Christ into a kitchen utensil. Jesus, in all His mosaic glory, hand to chest, looks like a whisk. And that's how "Eggbeater Jesus" was born. For more than fifty years, He's been mixing up omelets on the corner of Governors Drive.

That mosaic is so popular, its image has been turned into T-shirts and coffee mugs with the cheerful and hilarious caption: "Huntsville—Whisk you were here!"

It's the perfect combination of culture and camp, and you better believe I have one.

Unfortunately, with the passing of time, the mosaic started to sag and its tiles came loose, and eventually...they fell. One at a time, and then hundreds of tiles a day, little bits of blue and orange and yellow tumbling down from the FBC cosmos. Some bits landed on frozen gray bouffants as they made their way into the church. This happened so frequently that some of the elders joked they should start carrying umbrellas to the sanctuary. I find that detail particularly funny, but First Baptist Church was facing a real problem.

Cosmic Christ was falling to pieces, right there in front of God and everybody.

CHAPTER 3

Church Hurt

Let's rewind a little bit to the late 1900s (as my kids like to say) when I was a well-traveled soul in the musty-scented corridors of the Third Baptist Church of Dothan, Alabama. I was leading worship and driving my fish-stickered Honda to church every Wednesday and two times on Sunday.

I was a full-fledged Jesus Freak at the absolute peak of what is now known as the Purity Culture movement. If you know, you know; but if you don't, let me tell you: It was a challenging time to be a hormonal adolescent. Even worse if you were sinful enough to grow boobs. I can't tell you how many times I was pulled aside and asked to change clothes because my teenage body caused grown men to "stumble." I learned to wear multiple sports bras and baggy shirts, and to start slumping my shoulders.

I will never forget buying matching bathing suits with my friend Christen for the beach retreat. She was waifish and I was... not. But still, the exact same bathing suit. We had to get our attire "approved" in advance, because God forbid some fourteen-year-old boy catch wood for a sister in Christ. So, before we went swimming, we were to be inspected by a chaperone, like some ham at the county fair. Sigh. The exclusively feminine experience of having your form examined by a grown adult to determine whether or not just living in your body was going to be a problem for your "brothers in Christ." Anyways, Christen's suit got the green light. Mine did not. The only difference was the body I was born with.

I spent the entire retreat with a T-shirt thrown over that adorable teal one-piece. But that didn't stop me from finding a boyfriend and making out on the bus ride home. Turns out, it doesn't matter if you're wearing a plunging neckline or a potato sack, hormones are gonna keep hormoning. Of course, we felt shame for our sinful nature. We suppressed it, until he couldn't anymore, and that was the end of our romance.

Not one year later, the Third Baptist girls were invited to attend a True Love Waits rally—a daylong conference dedicated to teaching youth about sexual purity. Since I'd been marinating in sin since our beach retreat, I figured I'd better sign up.

I will never forget the keynote speaker holding up a single pink rose. So beautiful, so fragrant, so pure, he told us. Then he passed it around the church for all of us to admire. After the rose passed through a hundred or more hands, the speaker brought it back onstage and held it up for everyone to see. The rose had wilted. He claimed it was less fragrant. The once pristine petals were dull and dingy. While the rose had originally been a flower someone would receive with the sort of grin that shows all the teeth, it now looked like something you might find littering the sidewalk. A rose found on the ground that you know was a prop in someone's sad story. After being passed through so many hands, it was forever and irreversibly tainted.

The girls sat in uncomfortable silence as the weight of this message sank in.

Holy crap, are we that rose?

Who the heck wants a wilted, stinky flower?

Nobody. That was the answer.

It was crystal clear to all in attendance that our purity made us matter. Without it, we would have nothing to offer and no path to being loved. Our sexuality was a prize for our future husbands—it belonged to nobody else.

Except, apparently, our father figures?

The whole thing culminated in the creepiest ceremony ever. At the end of the night, after all of that shame, the boys were dismissed from the conference. While they went to the gym (to play basketball, I'm dead serious), the girls' fathers were escorted into another room. In this sort of junior wedding ritual, each girl's father presented her with a purity ring. A band that stood in as a placeholder for the ring we would receive when ownership transferred to our future husbands. Most of the girls accepted their purity ring with delight, the heaviness of the moment not sinking in for the majority of us. And then we made a promise—in writing, which was witnessed by our fathers—to remain sexually pure until marriage.

It was exactly as awful as it sounds. I'm sure everyone involved still has trauma. But my trauma was compounded by the fact that my first and former stepfather, Kenny—the man who put a ring on my finger, and whom I pledged my purity to—was the same damn person who had sexually abused me since I was in second grade.

That ring might as well have been made with fire, the way it burned into my skin. Signaling to the world that this man, my abuser, was the unofficial owner of my body.

Things got more complicated when, a little while later, I found myself falling in love. Not "back of the church bus make-out session" love. But the kind that was a little bit more meaningful. Rooted in friendship, and some big physical feelings. Evan wasn't from my youth group at all. In fact, his parents were agnostic. He was the first person to ever look at my ring with concern and ask some hard-hitting questions. Fellowship and living in a bubble is a big reason why things like purity rings can exist—it doesn't seem weird if everyone around you is doing it. Evan offered me a promise ring if I would take the damn thing off.

That night, we had our first fight. Because he was right; it was weird. Not regular weird, where you make an awkward face and walk away. The type of weird that hits you in your core with how not okay it is and glues your feet to the floor. It struck a deep nerve with me. Because deep down, I knew none of this was okay, but I wasn't willing to go into why. I couldn't reconcile my stepdad holding a signed pledge for my purity while being the one to destroy it. And I couldn't understand so much value being assigned to a thing that I had so very little control over protecting.

Eventually, we got around to talking about sex. About marriage. Because those two conversations go hand in hand in the majority of Southern towns. Most Christian teens have those talks with a mix of excitement and guilt. Me? I felt only one thing, and I felt it intensely.

Shame.

Shame that I had nothing of value to give to this guy. In my mind, I was ruined. I felt it seared into my skin like a scarlet letter for everyone to see, and it was going to cost me everything when Evan inevitably found out. Here was this amazing person who was caring and supportive and kind. What could I possibly offer him? Surely, he deserved better than a shame-ridden, wilted rose.

To the everlasting credit of this tenth-grade boy, Evan pulled me close and held me tight. He told me that despite what my church was teaching about the Bible commanding my purity, some biblical concepts couldn't work when applied literally to every single life situation. He told me that it was all too black-and-white, too unyielding, too literal to function in the gray. He told me he loved me; that nothing was broken. That a loving God wouldn't punish me for something I had absolutely zero control over.

What he said felt true, but I knew what the Bible said, and I just couldn't make it make sense. If Scripture was to be taken literally—and I believed that it was—there weren't any exceptions written into these chapters. Not even for victims like me.

I wasn't ready to report anything, but he nudged me repeatedly because he had the good sense to know I wouldn't be safe while that man remained in my home. He knew the abuse and violence would never stop on its own, and in my heart, I knew it, too. Together, we made a plan. I would wait for when I knew my stepdad would be away. Evan told me to find someone I trusted at my church, and I immediately thought of my Sunday school teacher. She was a friend of my mom's and a steady presence in my childhood. Truthfully, she was practically family, and I knew I could depend on her.

The only problem: My abuser was a deacon.

So we bided our time, Sunday after Sunday, until, finally, deer season came. The very first weekend he was out of town hunting, I told my Sunday school teacher everything. At least, everything I could. She believed me, thank God, but when she tried to get details, I couldn't give her much. I didn't have the language to describe what happened to me. Because of Purity Culture, I felt deeply uncomfortable using words like "penis" or "vagina." I had no idea what some of the acts were even called, but trying to find the words was humiliating. Not only was I reliving my trauma, but I felt like every piece I tried to share got me pelted with more and more shame and self-loathing.

My teacher retrieved my mother from her Sunday school class. My mom listened to what happened, and she looked at me, then at my teacher, and then back at me. As a mother, I think about the moments that followed and I can feel the injury I saw on my mom's face. She was devastated. Both for what I had gone through and that the trusted adult I had chosen wasn't her. I don't mean that she was upset with me or feeling bad on her own behalf. The pain she felt was for me and that I hadn't been able to come to her first. Sooner. That her child didn't feel safe.

Within twenty-four hours, he was arrested and booked. His belongings were processed as evidence. In his wallet: $20, his license, a Blockbuster card, and my True Love Waits purity pledge card.

A few days later, my stepfather was released on bail, and my family was advised to get out of town. For two weeks, I was put up in a Florida hotel as the story hit the Alabama news circuit. Not that child abuse is a typically hot news topic, but the thing was—he was also a cop. And not just any cop, but captain of the SWAT team, beloved by his fellow officers, and thus had the nickname "Boy Scout." To the police, my community, and also my church, my abuser was considered a saint.

Eventually, my family was told to come home. Our house had been armed with security and a phone that was wired directly to dispatch. Apparently, "Boy Scout," the Third Baptist Church deacon, was considered a threat to my life. I wish I could say that this threat stayed only a threat, but for the next several years, we were terrorized. Our home was broken into; shots were fired from outside and a bullet was embedded in the dining room wall. On my sixteenth birthday, I caught my abuser crawling in through the kitchen window. I ran down the hall screaming, locked myself in the bathroom, and called the police on our hotline.

I'd like to tell you that the entire police force showed up with sirens blazing. But that would be a lie, and I'd rather tell the truth—which is ugly, so buckle yourselves up. Not only did the police not arrive in a hurry, they didn't arrive for an hour. The entire time, I sat curled up behind the toilet, shivering from terror and screaming at dispatch, while my abuser paced outside the door, laughing and mocking my terror. I knew he had a gun, and if he wanted to, he'd shoot. Our dining room wall was proof of that fact. But I also knew that the very same dining room bullet, which was supposed to be tested for ballistics, had gotten "lost" in the processing. It would never be found. The police (and most of our small town) had clearly chosen their side. Boy Scout was the victim, and I was a liar.

I prayed that I'd make it to trial.

When the SWAT team finally did arrive, the house was empty and the kitchen window was shattered. Boot prints were in the kitchen sink, and glass was all over the house. My friend Randy, who was supposed to pick me up to celebrate my birthday, had been pulling into the driveway, unaware of the crisis unfolding inside. The poor kid was held for questioning. My abuser not only routinely escaped the consequences of his actions; he didn't even suffer the inconveniences.

After that, understandably, a whole lot of parents weren't super comfortable with their kids hanging out with me. Now, as a mom, I understand their decisions. I'm not sure I'd have done anything different. My situation was dangerous, all over the news, and affected my friendships. But as a child and a victim, this was a devastating blow. The well of support I was drawing upon had dried up with incredible speed.

Except, thank God, I still had my church. For all its flaws, TBC did all right...at first. My stepdad had been removed as a deacon. The pastor had come to pray for me. My Sunday school teacher had immediately believed me. Church, I believed, was my safe place.

And then, I signed up for church league basketball. It was a way to stay busy and make friends. Also, I was a horrendous basketball player, and church league was the only place I could cut it. I remember my excitement the first day of practice, lacing up my shoes at the Family Life Center. The FLC was a church-owned gym that, apparently, also sold memberships. I didn't know this until I was halfway through practice and taking a water break. I was bent over the water fountain, chugging in earnest, when I felt a large presence behind me. Thinking someone must've been reeeeally thirsty, I took one final gulp and stood up. Wiping my chin, I turned back around, and practically ran into my stepdad.

No words were exchanged, but the look on his face said it all. *You will never escape me.*

I ran from the gym, straight to my car, and peeled out of the parking lot as if the building were on fire. When I ran into the house, uncontrollably sobbing, my mom asked what was the matter. So I told her. "Kenny was at the FLC. He was working out there during basketball."

General Sherman had nothing on my mother the day she marched into that church. She was on a warpath, and a righteous one, too. But our pastor was shocked by her outrage.

He had already removed Boy Scout from the deacon list. Wasn't that punishment enough? What was he supposed to do? Ban this man from the premises?

Yes, my mother informed that man. That's exactly what he should do.

Eventually, the pastor agreed with my mom and banned my abuser from the gym. But "with love," he strongly suggested our family consider some Christian counseling. Maybe, he said, it would be good for us all to work through this trauma with support. Even better, the counselor he recommended could bill on a sliding scale. And since Mom was now alone, trying to make ends meet, and wanting her daughter to heal...she agreed.

After all, this was a Christian counselor. What would it hurt to try?

I agreed with mom that I needed more therapy. The Child Advocacy Center offered free support, but their availability was limited (a heartbreaking statement about the prevalence of this issue—and please, donate to this organization). Anyways, I asked for a couple of sessions, eager to give it a shot.

Walking into the office of Mr. Christian Counselor, everything was so safe and warm. So many pillows, encouraging posters, pictures of a white, smiling Jesus. He sat down across a round table from me, which was new, but I didn't hate it. I also didn't hate that he was hot and a dead ringer for Viggo Mortensen. Not sure if I knew who that was at the time, but I do now, and the point still stands.

"I have a worksheet for you to fill out," he said. "It might help us jump-start the conversation."

I wanted nothing more than to make him proud, so I grabbed a pen and started answering questions.

Are you holding on to anger? Yes. I'm pissed. C'mon, I was fucking abused. (I didn't write that because I was a youth group kid. But, whatever I said, I'm 100 percent sure that I pressed the pen down extra hard when I wrote it.)

What is the best way to move forward from anger? I don't know; that's actually why I am here.

Have you considered forgiveness as a path to freedom?

I dropped my pen on the table.

"I'm sorry...but, I'm confused by this question. Is this worksheet for everyone that comes in? Are...are you suggesting I forgive my abuser?"

"You came here looking for a path to healing. Forgiveness is that path."

He smiled that Aragorn smile.

And, suddenly, I didn't trust it.

In that moment, something shifted in me. This counselor, with all his warm decor and platitudes, didn't feel like the safe haven that was advertised. Even as a child, I couldn't accept the idea that I'd find healing by forcing forgiveness, which it sure seemed this counselor was suggesting. What about accountability? What about recompense?

I stopped going to see that counselor, but I still longed for belonging in the church. I needed that anchor in my life, however flawed, and I hoped that one day I would find a place in the faith where I could truly feel safe and at home. I carried that hope forward through the next several years, still longing for a genuine faith community. One that would mend my wide-open wounds, not stick a dirty finger inside of them.

I grew up, went to college, failed out of college (more on that later), became a missionary, came home, and eventually met my husband, Ian.

At first, I was drawn to his unique worldview. He had a childlike sense of humor and wasn't afraid to boldly criticize the politics and culture I'd grown up entrenched in. He questioned things I had always accepted as truth, and while I didn't always agree with him, I found it fascinating. His off-kilter fashion—European-inspired with slim-cut pants, highlights in his hair, and earrings in both ears—stood in sharp contrast to the boys I grew up with. It wasn't a "bad boy" look, but it was different, and maybe that's what excited me. I didn't quite understand him, and that mystery felt fresh and exhilarating.

We fell in love quickly, swept up in what felt like a whirlwind of connection and shared faith. But looking back, I wonder how much of it was driven by the beliefs we were raised with. We grew up praying for our future spouses, believing that God would send us someone who would complete us. We were taught to wait, to hold out for this divine partnership, and that marriage would be the fulfillment of all those prayers.

We were both cookie-cutter stamps of the Purity Culture movement—purity rings, youth group pledges, and all the metaphors about chewed gum, wilted roses, and cows giving away free milk. And yet, we struggled to wait. Our engagement came quickly, and within a year of dating, we were married. At the time, it felt like the only way forward—not just because we loved each other, but because we believed marriage would save us from ourselves and from our desires.

We got married and threw ourselves into church life, trying to piece together our faith and our marriage, as if one could fix the other.

A few years later, Ian graduated from medical school and it was time to leave Huntsville behind. (*For now*, I kept telling myself. *Not forever.*) I was terrified of leaving my home state. But he'd been matched with a residency in Orlando, Florida, and it was time for a new life adventure. So, we packed up our home and our two stinky dogs and started driving on I-65. It was gonna be awesome! Mickey Mouse. Sunshine. Less than an hour to the beach. And if I missed my family, I could always get home. The direct flights were fairly reasonable.

At least, that's what I kept telling myself every time the anxiety kicked in.

I was still very much a small-town girl with a conservative perspective to draw from when we rolled into that big, sunny city with a carful of clothes and two dogs.

I did my best to settle into the Sunshine State while Ian got busy working. This was the *Grey's Anatomy* phase of Ian's training, meaning long hours and a whole lot of stress. It was lonely, not having him home very much, in a city that swallowed me whole. In Alabama, I'd grown up in a world where everyone knew your name and the names of your parents. You didn't really have to worry about weekend plans, because on any given Saturday a family member was hosting a barbecue or a kid's birthday party. I'd grown attached to this small-town simple life, so Orlando was a big change.

At first, I'd been excited about my new corporate job with a commercial real estate developer. I had a pretty corner office in a high-rise building that overlooked a lake with a fountain. But that nine-to-five grind didn't quite fill my soul in the way my hometown life had.

I did, however, find a church just a couple of blocks from the bungalow we rented. I did my best to connect with the church's young adult ministry, but that was a challenge, too. Ian was in his trauma surgery rotation, and his pager was constantly buzzing. So, I went by myself to a Sunday school class full of hand-holding, snuggled-up newlyweds. And though they were lovely and did their best to include me, the whole situation only made me more lonely.

"I'll never make friends in this town," I sobbed over the phone to my mom one night. "I'm going to church and I'm trying to make friends, but I've never felt so alone."

Momma assured me that God would provide. And the next day at work, I met Michael.

He had a brilliant smile and a Southern drawl and he sounded a whole lot like home. We started talking at work.

Soon, I was picking up his favorite latte on the way to work. And on our lunch breaks, he would gush all about the love of his life, Jesse. I assumed Jesse was a girl, but that assumption turned out to be wrong. When we all met for lunch one day, I couldn't conceal my shock.

"Oh my GOSH, Michael! You're gay?"

"Um, DUH." He laughed. "Did the cowboy hat throw you off?"

I then remembered he had recently pointed out a bar a few blocks from my house. He mentioned that it was a fun place to go, and I replied that one day we should…but I hadn't noticed the rainbow details.

"MK, your gaydar isn't malfunctioning. It's completely nonexistent."

Michael and Jesse told me funny stories about drag contests and bouncers who wore shorty shorts. They insisted I would love Thursday night karaoke, but I assured them it wasn't my scene.

I blushed and giggled a little at the idea.

It sounded fun, if not a bit scandalous.

A week or so after that hilarious lunch date, I was driving home from a friend's house one night, right past that same gay bar Michael had pointed out to me, when I witnessed a young lady being struck by a car. I swerved to the side of the road and jumped out of my vehicle, screaming.

In an instant, people poured out of the bar to assist in the emergency. I barely registered that they were dressed flamboyantly. Their makeup didn't strike me as strange. In that moment, we were all scared human beings. Their hearts were racing just like mine.

A drag queen cradled the woman's head in his hands as I called the police.

"Don't move, baby girl," he comforted the woman. "Don't mess up these pretty braids."

It was a fraction of a moment that felt like forever. I can still hear her crying for Momma. Thankfully, the club was only a block from the hospital, and the ambulance arrived in an instant.

When the lights and sirens finally faded, my adrenaline-filled body couldn't handle silence. It was like every one of us had been shaken like soft drinks, and in that moment, we had all cracked open. There were hugs and prayers exchanged between strangers. I remember someone humming a hymn.

Then slowly, one by one, the crowd dispersed. We had to go back to our lives. But not before exchanging a couple of phone numbers, promising to share any updates.

I called my friends Michael and Jesse. I understood that the gay community in Orlando was a close one and I wondered if they'd heard any news.

Michael asked around, but he didn't hear much.

"Don't worry," he said. "We will know more tomorrow."

I decided to stay up until then.

The next morning, we all went to breakfast with the drag queens, who had started a text thread for updates. We bonded over hash browns and our collective trauma—and after coffee, just some regular life stories.

The woman, we learned, was in critical condition. Two broken legs and a fractured spine. James, who had cradled her head so gently, had probably saved her life. Turns out, he had done so with great intention because not only was he a drag queen, but once a month he returned to his rural hometown to serve as a medic for the volunteer fire department.

A hero. An absolute gem of a human.

I decided to invite James to church. To my delight (and a bit of surprise), he accepted my invitation.

For the next few months, James showed up to church with a Starbucks cup in each hand. A skinny vanilla latte for me and a white chocolate mocha for him. We'd sip our drinks at that big round table, laughing with the rest of the Sunday school class. James had a knack for presenting Scripture in a way that spurred deep, theological discussions. We'd discuss the day's lesson, share our personal struggles, and at the end of class, pray for one another.

And then one day, after closing prayer, James said that he'd like to get baptized. He filled out an interest card for the church, requesting new member information. I decided that I should fill one out, too, since it'd been awhile since I was dunked. I figured it'd be more special together, and, after all, I was due for a re-up.

That week, we individually received invitations to meet with the church's lead pastor. I went first at 1:00 p.m., and the whole thing went pretty smoothly. Just the basics of a Southern Baptist sign-up.

Do you love Jesus? Do you understand sin? Did you ask Jesus into your heart?

I was in and out of that office in minutes, a card-carrying congregation member. James was supposed to be one hour behind me, so I expected his call at any moment. But the hours kept ticking, and James didn't call. By dinnertime, I was growing concerned.

First I texted. Then I called.

Then I started to panic. A day went by, and then a couple more days. At this point, I was worrying myself sick.

I reached out to Michael, who had no idea what was happening but was happy to meet for coffee.

"Babe, I don't really know him that well. But if I had to guess…that meeting with your Southern Baptist pastor didn't go so smoothly for James."

A familiar knot of doubt started to form in my stomach. I knew the Bible verses used to condemn same-sex relationships by heart—the "clobber verses," as they're called. And I'd heard the usual explanations in church about how "homosexuality is a sin" and about "God's design for marriage."

But those verses…could they mean something different? I had read about more-loving translations that aligned with Christ's teachings on compassion and inclusion, but to entertain that idea felt like questioning the Bible itself, something I felt I was not allowed to do. I had always managed to push those thoughts aside. You have to understand, Christianity wasn't just my faith; it was my culture, my community, and a lens I had used to understand the world for as long as I could remember. Living inside that system, I had developed a kind of cognitive dissonance.

James was gay, and he was also a wonderful human being who loved God and wanted to be part of a church, and I couldn't reconcile that truth with the things I'd always been told about gay people being bad. So...I just didn't. I tucked those conflicting beliefs far away in some corner at the back of my mind so I wouldn't have to face my own questions.

I didn't consciously do this. It's just that I'd done it so many times that I forgot what it felt like to question it. I had long since swallowed the contradictions between what the church said and what I experienced in my actual life. I'd been taught that the world would lie to me, and that what the church taught was the only truth. I'd learned to keep my blinders on to make it all work.

Michael shook his head like he knew a sad secret that he didn't really want to share. Luckily, he didn't have to. Because that's when I heard back from James.

> Hey Sugar Bear. Sorry I disappeared. Rough week.
> Not really your fault. I met with the pastor, and it didn't
> work out. Not coming back. Please understand.
>
> XOXO, James

I blinked for a minute, just staring at the screen. What did he mean, "It didn't work out"? James had been welcomed at church every Sunday—what did the pastor say?

With furious tears welling up in my eyes, I stood up in the middle of Starbucks.

"I'm going to the church. I'm gonna talk to the pastor."

"Right now?" Michael asked.

"Right. Now."

Michael squeezed me tight and wished me good luck, but I was certain that I wouldn't need it.

"This is all some sort of misunderstanding," I said.

"I hope so," was all he replied.

And as I left, I noticed his eyes were still holding on to that secret.

A few hours later, I left Pastor Mark's office with an angry and broken heart. I'd received an up-front-and-personal education on the difference between acceptance and inclusion. According to the pastor, James was living in sin and therefore could not be a member of the church. To be clear, James was welcome to attend Sunday school, to bond with and pray over members. He was encouraged to tithe, volunteer, and attend. None of that was a problem. But when it came to the official act of joining, my church held a thick red line. James was gay, and therefore condemned. He was not a "true" brother in Christ.

Looking back now, I realize this moment was one of the many, many times I'd felt an internal struggle to reconcile my values of love and kindness with the teachings of the beliefs I espoused. All those years as a front-row Baptist, and I still didn't see what was in front of me. There was a long list of casualties from the zillion pileups that occurred at the intersection of evangelical Christianity and queer identity.

Seeing what happened with James, the inconsistencies were becoming harder to ignore. I started questioning whether the

Jesus I read about in Scripture—the one who always sided with the overlooked and misunderstood—was the same person I sang praise choruses about in that church. But even as these questions surfaced, I wasn't ready to confront the deeper patterns. I wasn't ready to face what it might mean if this was not just one isolated failure but something bigger, woven into the fabric of evangelical theology itself.

Instead, I clung to an easier explanation. I told myself this was just one bad pastor, one broken church, one act of injustice. It wasn't the theology itself that was flawed; I just needed to find a healthier spiritual community. Like dating, I thought, I'd eventually find the "right" church, one that truly loved me and the whole world well. I'd settle down there, and my faith would heal. It was comforting to think that all this hate and harm was simply proof I'd trusted the wrong people. The system wasn't the problem—it was just this particular expression of it.

So I withdrew my membership and drove home, clinging to the belief that it wasn't the theology, just *this* church. But before I walked through the door, I texted James.

> I am so sorry. I know I can't do anything to make this better, but I really am sorry.

I never heard from James again, but I did hear something of that pastor.

Many years later, he was caught having an extramarital affair, and he exited the ministry for good.

CHAPTER 4

New Hope

Two years after I withdrew my membership from that church in Orlando, Ian graduated from residency and our family moved south to Fort Myers. We'd had a baby by this point, and in the throes of new motherhood, I hadn't really gone back to church, but now I started looking for a church that would welcome us in. With tired eyes, one very loud baby, and a mildly desperate need to connect with other adults, it was harder than we anticipated to find a church home. (You'd be surprised how many churches hate babies. God forbid, they actually cry.)

Anyways, if you've ever dated in any sort of way (seeking a lover, a therapist, a new ob-gyn), you know how that process can be.

Awkward. Vulnerable. Scary. Humbling.

It's so many things all at once.

Well, when you're dating a church, it's a bit more complicated because it's not just you on the date. You're dressing up your children and prodding along your spouse and praying they all act right, then walking through those double doors into...well, only God knows what.

Once, when I was visiting a megachurch in Texas, the service opened up with an enormous TV screen showing a helicopter landing. On live TV, we watched as the pastor rappelled onto the roof of the church, wearing head-to-toe camo. The cameras followed him all the way backstage where, and I sincerely wish I were joking, a whole-ass military tank was waiting for him. And yes, he drove it onto the stage.

The sermon was about the armor of God. I'm not sure where the chopper fit in.

After a few similar horrors, I learned to check the website of a church before paying a visit. Sometimes those red flags are buried in the fine print, but sometimes? They're the feature presentation. Turns out, if I'd done a quick Google search of that megachurch, I'd have known they were famous for such stunts. I'd made the mistake of thinking a full parking lot was evidence of a healthy community.

It was a mistake I didn't make twice.

After weeks of scouring local church websites, I found one that gave me some hope. It was aptly named "New Hope." No tanks, no choppers, no condemning the marginalized. Their mantra: Unity in the essentials. Grace in the nonessentials.

I believed that meant all my friends would be welcomed and loved. Included, not just accepted.

So, I decided to give it a shot. And soon enough, I was falling in love. New Hope was a quaint congregation, but I could feel that it had a big heart. And even better, they had excellent programming. There was a MOPS (Mothers of Preschoolers) group, which I instantly joined. They offered incredible support. Every week, I met with other women who were navigating parenthood in the same stage as me. It was a community I desperately needed, and, frankly, it felt like a balm to my heart. Meanwhile, Ben was overcoming his separation anxiety and thriving in the children's program. The sermons were safe, my kid was happy, and Sunday school was always an encouragement.

For a number of years, that "unity in essentials" was just what the doctor ordered.

But then something happened in 2016. It was called a "presidential election," but it didn't really act like one. Or maybe it did, and this is America, now.

I'd like to think that's not the case.

Anyways, for months, the entirety of social media was just people going for one another's throats. It was ugly and polarizing, and there were crowds cheering it on, but they were cheering it on like a rooster fight. As if it weren't something that was actively breaking up families and ruining lives.

For the most part, our church stayed quiet about all of these things. It was weird, like a bad family secret. There was tension. It was vague, but very much present. It changed the whole vibe in the room. You know that feeling you get when you're a little kid and you run into a room for a snack, and your parents are in there, and nobody's talking, but you know for a fact they've been fighting?

Weird, but calm. That's what it was.

In a way, I prefer it to be loud.

Trump was elected, and a few months later I was asked to help lead the praise band. To be honest, that made me feel special. Feel seen. So I stayed through the weird and the calm. I thought we had weathered the storm okay, by avoiding the subject completely. Even though I should've known better, I believed that the silence was safe. Of course this was in 2019, right around the time my son asked the question that sparked my deconstruction journey. I'd tried to bury that seed of doubt, but it sprouted quickly, and by 2020, when a global pandemic hit, doubt had just about taken over the garden.

A little context: Ian was by this point an emergency room physician. He was on the first line of responders when shit hit the fan—and COVID hit every single freaking fan.

It was a terrifying time to be married to someone in the medical field, particularly someone in the trenches. Sometimes, it felt like he got home from work, took a shower, and went right back in. The hospital system where he was employed was struggling to find PPE (personal protective equipment). All medical provisions were in short supply as Fort Myers became known as a "hot spot."

Every day, Ian showed up to serve in a hospital that looked and felt like a war zone. Around every corner was something loud and terrible. A contagious cough, a machine going haywire as somebody's stats started crashing, an intubation team hollering orders, the wail of a brand-new widow.

There were people whose families couldn't be with them as they died while begging to see their loved ones. And loved ones who couldn't say goodbye to their families, screaming at helpless employees. All day, every day, Ian saw the most terrible things, delivered the most terrible news, and did it all in a mask that was ten days old (and nine days past its effectiveness).

Inevitably, Ian tested positive for COVID. We knew it would happen eventually. It was scary, because he was really sick. That early strain was unpredictably deadly, and in this time frame there was no treatment or defense. You just caught it and died, or if you caught it and didn't die, you decided if you believed it was real.

It was honestly the most insane time. And then it got worse. Because then I got it.

Two parents, in two separate rooms, with two rowdy children under the age of five. Ben and Holland could barely wipe their own butts, much less bathe and cook their own meals. There was zero treatment and no way to gauge our prognoses. Our community was far too terrified to help. I understood why they felt that way.

After fifteen days with a fever of 103, my temperature spiked, my oxygen tanked, and I was rushed to my husband's ER. The one he had not yet returned to, because he was still infected, with our children, at home.

It was the most terrifying illness of my life, and that's saying something because I'm a breast cancer survivor. The medical environment is one I'm well acquainted with, from Ian's work as well as my own complicated history.

But COVID was like nothing I'd ever experienced. I guess that's why it was called "novel."

I couldn't breathe. My fever kept spiking and my brain was on fire. No medication was helping. Our next-door neighbor, Jeff, was also a doctor who worked in the unit where I was kept. He couldn't come and hang out at my bedside, as much as I knew he wanted to. He could only talk to me through layers of plastic sheeting, over the roar of air purification systems and oxygen tanks.

I remember thinking this must have been what it was like for E.T. in that government hazmat tent, everyone too afraid to get close because who knew what ailment from outer space he could transmit. Feeling like I had been dropped into the scariest part of the movie didn't exactly lift my spirits. I was isolated, alone, and incredibly sick. Ten out of ten, I do not recommend almost dying from a novel virus.

Imagine my surprise when I was finally released to continue my recovery at home, only to pop onto the internet and find out through my church friends that I was confused and tricked about this whole COVID situation. It wasn't real, this pandemic. It was just some device in an Orwellian agenda to kill all the good guys and microchip everybody else.

I'm sorry, what? I couldn't believe my eyes.

But there it was, right on my screen. On Facebook and Instagram and text messages. The people I sat alongside at church were angrily, loudly, bitterly railing against what they dubbed fake news.

There were endless posts trashing any cautionary measures being taken by local governments. There were proclamations about "rights" and "persecution." There was a group on Facebook called Christian Moms Against Masks who claimed that masking was literal child abuse.

It was like I left planet Earth when I went to the hospital and I exited into a strange new galaxy when I was released. Where up was down and fact was fiction and there was a new king named Joe Exotic.

Suddenly, these "brothers and sisters" of mine were taking swipes at my character and faith. Making blanket statements about our beliefs that left me outside the covers.

I was heartbroken when I realized "unity in the essentials" meant we agreed only on Jesus. Seriously, end of list. Because I consider basic decency to be somewhat essential, and for these brethren, it clearly was not.

"Grace in the nonessentials" apparently meant that I was expected to tolerate Sunday school friends who really wanted me to watch *Plandemic* while I was recovering from this "fake" virus.

"Grace in the nonessentials" meant scrolling past post after post from people I thought loved my family, but who were raging against health-care workers who were supposedly "in on the whole thing." And this while my husband was struggling to breathe.

And I was supposed to commune with these folks? Make them my spiritual support system?

The "essentials" essentially went down the drain as I saw plainly what was in front of me. The pandemic loaded my illusion of church onto E.T.'s ship and launched it right into outer space. I know many who felt the same way that year. I know many who've felt it for decades. But for me, it was new, and it scared me to death. I didn't want to let go. I clung like hell to any shred of hope that this beloved community could be salvaged.

It's okay, I thought. *We'll get past this, and we'll go back to kinder ways. We'll drop the declarations and the false assumptions. It'll be fine. It will go back to fine.*

Even as I tried to convince myself things would go back to "fine," I was still wrestling with big questions about my faith—about hell, salvation, who gets left out. I kept trying to push these questions down, telling myself they weren't urgent. After all, we were supposed to be unified on the "essentials." That idea alone was my lifeline. I thought if I could just hang on, this community would go back to what I needed it to be.

I sorta kinda convinced myself this was possible.

But it only got worse and worse.

Inevitably, these relationships were added to the list of casualties COVID racked up. In the coming decades, when anthropologists study the harm that this pandemic caused, I believe the loss of life will be impossible to truly quantify.

I say this because we all lost someone, even if that someone didn't die. We lost community with people we once trusted. We lost respect for those who disappointed us most. We lost confidence in a society that couldn't get its shit together long enough to stop millions from dying. We lost sanity, because we were constantly being gaslit. We lost love; we lost people; we lost friendships.

The disease killed so many, but for the ones left behind, it revealed an entirely new problem—a pandemic that will prove even harder to fix.

Humanity lost its humanity.

And let me tell you, as someone who still had one foot in the door of evangelicalism, I was given an up-front seat to the horror of watching my church contract this illness.

With the depth of division growing at New Hope, I finally walked into the pastor's office and told him my concerns. I talked about the distress these members had caused me, given that I almost died. I recounted my concern that there were church leaders involved in many of these rants. Even an associate pastor.

I talked about the lack of kindness and compassion from those who claimed to be unified in the essentials, but who were now promoting a list of exclusionary clauses to our whole claim.

What I was told by church leadership was that there was nothing to worry about.

I needed to keep eating the crackers.

"We're unified on what matters, Mary Katherine. That's what's most important. We agree about Jesus."

I tried to let that statement digest, but it didn't feel like the whole truth. A whole lot of people "believe" in Jesus, but their actions are inarguably cruel. A pit was growing in the bottom of my stomach, an unsettling and familiar sensation. This felt very much like a breakup talk. Two perspectives, both strong and unmoving.

A part of me wanted to argue my point, to continue having this talk. But something deep inside my spirit compelled me to walk away. So I prayed with my pastor, wished him well, grabbed my Bible, and turned for the door. Ultimately, I couldn't "agree to disagree" on what felt like basic decency.

It seemed to me that "good Christian people" should at the very least be…good people.

· · · · · · · · · ·

In the year of our Lord 2024, Taylor Swift won the Super Bowl. So did her boyfriend, Travis Kelce, who I'm pretty sure played for the Chiefs. I don't actually remember who the losing team was and I'm sure they did a fine job. But there was way too much content in that one night of television for my brain to download it all. Filling the rest of that memory space was Usher in a crop top, dancing in roller skates, and a $21 million commercial about Jesus that was so hilariously misunderstood the phrase "Jesus was a foot guy" was trending online for three days after its airing.

If your first thought is *What kinda church spends millions of dollars on a PR stunt for Jesus?*, then hello, you are my people. I wondered the same thing, which is why I immediately went digging for more information.

On the surface, the commercial is pretty straightforward.

It opens with a carousel of images of modern people washing one another's feet. A police officer washing a Black man's feet. An older woman washing the feet of a teenage girl who was sitting outside an abortion clinic. A priest washing the feet of a gay Black man. You get the point. The images are touching.

The commercial ends with a blacked-out screen and a message in bright yellow words.

Jesus didn't teach hate.
He washed feet.
He gets us.
All of us.

The organization claims they wanted to "remind everyone, including ourselves, that Jesus' teachings are a warm embrace, not a cold shoulder."

However, it was a church with this exact kind of kumbaya Jesus that taught me to peek under the covers. So that's what I did, and what I found was disappointing (and, sadly, somewhat predictable).

Turns out, the groups behind this loving, inclusive message were not very loving or inclusive at all. Most of the funders were political lobbyists whose actions didn't jive with their message. That photo of a gay man was funded by a family who spent millions challenging gay marriage. That photo of the girl at an abortion clinic? Brought to you by the very same family who stripped their employees of reproductive-care insurance because they didn't support reproductive care.

Now, before you throw my book away, I'm not asking you to agree with my politics. Not in this book, anyways. I've been alive long enough to know that what I believe today I may not tomorrow. So, I've lost some rigidity there.

What bothered me most (aside from the price tag) was the fact that this commercial was directly appealing to the people that Christians hurt most. There is nothing more devastating than finding a safe place and then having it crumble around you.

· · · · · · · · · ·

All of this is why, when I walked out of that meeting with my pastor in Fort Myers, the one where he'd told me to overlook the hatred that was being directed at me weekly, I barely made it to my car before I hunkered down in sobs. I wasn't sure where the hurt was coming from, but it was coming in big, angry waves.

I punched my steering wheel. I screamed. I cried. I yelled the longest, most satisfying string of words that shouldn't be spoken at church, but I figured at this point that if Jesus was listening, He'd probably understand.

I'd invested so much of my heart, my time, and my resources into New Hope. But the first time I challenged the status quo, my stock value crashed just like that.

For the next little while, I sat in the parking lot, wiping away my own tears. I watched as the MOPS group let out and my friends poured out of the church, tugging their children along. Children I'd held as babies and watched grow. Whose mothers hosted my second baby shower. I watched as these women hopped into their minivans, driving off in a single-file line.

Who knew why this was my final breaking point, but looking back now, I see that it was. I was done with church. It could all go to hell—if hell was even a place.

When the dust settles after a breakup, I've sometimes been afforded enough perspective to see the difference between the reality I built for myself and actual, real reality. That this devastating blow that initially felt like it came out of nowhere was actually a long time coming. That the happy, safe, loving community that was supposed to last forever had, in reality, led to a death by a thousand cuts. A series of seemingly small but not insignificant hurts that weren't big enough on their own to feel consequential, but added up to a picture very different from the one I had painted.

Maybe it's just what happens when you put your faith in something fragile—whether it's a community or a partnership. When the cracks start to show, it's easier to explain them away than to ask what they mean. Until, of course, it all falls apart.

Looking back, I can see that my relationship with the church had never been sunshine and roses. My friends in Sunday school colored their Noah's ark pictures, and I colored mine, too. But I did it with some conflicting feelings about everyone who hadn't been on that boat, people and animals both. Later, the story of

Abraham being commanded to sacrifice one of his sons twisted my stomach so bad that I tried to block it from my brain when I started having my own babies. The thought of that command was probably the only thing more terrible to me than hell. If I thought on it too much, reconciling a God that loves us with a God who would inflict that greatest possible agony onto a parent would surely lead me to hell, where I could think about it some more.

My experience at New Hope may have been the catalyst for the breakup. But the red flags had been there all along. I had just lacked the perspective to recognize them for what they were, and I overlooked what I didn't want to see.

I was done with my abusive relationship with church. No more choking on horse pills of forgiveness. There was nothing left in my stomach to bear it; nothing left to chase it down. No more looking the other way while people I loved were treated like they didn't matter. No more pretending that people could be excluded for who they were and still call it love. After decades of hurt and patterns of abuse, it had finally occurred to me…The church wasn't sorry. And they didn't want my forgiveness either. What they wanted was my complicity. A shut mouth and a butt on the pew.

Wiping away the last of my tears, I shifted my car into drive, then I drove away from that church for the millionth (and very last) time.

I'm not sure if you knew this or not, but Alabama is in Tornado Alley. I know, we all grew up with the Wizard of Oz notion that the Great Plains held this distinction. But as the climate continues to change, so, too, have the patterns and severity of storms. So, for the last thirty years, Tornado Alley has been tiptoeing farther and farther south. Growing up in Alabama means familiarizing yourself with terminology like "vortex" and "safe space" and "polygon." I'm not joking when I say that in these parts, our meteorologist is as beloved as Dolly Parton. When James Spann rolls up his sleeves, all of Alabama knows it's time to go to the basement.

On January 21, 2010, a tornado touched down in Huntsville. Ian and I were still living in the Medical District, in a home with an underground basement. Which would have been great, if that's where I went, but I regret to admit I did not. Dear Lord, I hope that James Spann doesn't read this because I was not respecting the polygon.

You know those rednecks who are interviewed by the news after a tornado hits? The ones who are like "Welp, I thought I heard a train so I went outside, then it picked me up and shooook me like a dawg!"

I'm ashamed to say that could've been me.

To be fair (not that this is in any way justified), I'd had a couple of cocktails. My cousin and a few friends had come over for dinner and after a cosmo or two, those alarms started blazing and with liquor as courage, we went outside like a bunch of drunk storm chasers.

Now, I'd lived through quite a few storms at this point, but when I looked up, I 'bout wet my pants. Because right there, with Eggbeater Jesus in the foreground, was a cloud-to-ground whole-ass tornado. Just google "Eggbeater Jesus tornado," and you'll see what I saw from my driveway. We ran inside, hunkered down in the basement, and started praying like inmates on death row.

It was right around this time that it was decided Eggbeater Jesus was facing a crisis. Okay, actually, the crisis was His face. Thousands of tiles had fallen from the mosaic, leaving large swaths of gray, empty patches. It looked like Jesus had a bad case of leprosy, and that wasn't part of the story.

So the church commissioned study after study to research each point of failure. In an interview with the local news, Pastor Travis Collins quipped, "This thing has been studied more than anything except the Bible around here."

Their hope was to repair the original mosaic, but hope was starting to grow thin. First came a tile guy, who said that the tiles didn't bond to the glue on the wall. Then came a glue guy, who said that the glue couldn't bond because of the moisture. Then came—I dunno, a moisture guy? All of these studies concluded with the same bad news: Jesus couldn't be fixed.

While Jesus was able to carry our sins, He couldn't weather our weather. A swift wind, or a storm, or the oppressive hot summers—all of it was too much for the Cosmic Christ. His foundation wasn't sticky enough. A slight wind could send bits of Him flying off the walls, to say nothing of Southern tornadoes.

If this church wanted a Jesus who could weather the storm, they'd have to stop patching up this one.

The whole dang thing was gonna have to come down.

CHAPTER 5

Doubting Thomas

A few months into my freshman year of college, my life had become one big party. I'd fully embraced the fun-filled life of a Southern sorority stereotype. I was kicking butt at intramural football, dating a cute frat boy, and even snagged a spot on the dance team. In my not-quite-fully-developed brain, I had my priorities sorted. Never mind that my GPA was so low it couldn't buy a small pack of chewing gum. Who cared about silly things like grades? I was having the time of my life!

Well, my dad cared a whole lot, thankyouverymuch. He wasn't gonna bankroll a party. So on a random Tuesday in the middle of the semester, my father got into his car and drove from Texas, where he lived, to Alabama to drag my crazy butt home with him. Believe me when I tell y'all he rolled in like SEAL Team 6, with nothing but a rolling suitcase. I was halfway to Dallas when my head stopped spinning long enough to process what had happened. As I sat in the car, watching the familiar landscape of my home state fade away, I couldn't help but feel a growing sense of disconnect—from my friends, from my life, and most of all…from God. I had believed so fervently before college, but now, the party scene had become my church. And that scared me more than I let on.

The eleven-hour drive was mostly silent. I felt angry, depressed, and ashamed. I knew his decision was just. But what was I going to tell my sorority sisters when they found my dorm room empty?

Before college, I had always been an honor roll student. I had never even tasted alcohol. But here I was, a hungover college flunk-out on a trip with my disappointed father. Within hours, my friends were spamming my phone with texts, asking just what the heck happened. As far as they knew, I'd been doing just fine, and this was some sort of family emergency. I decided I wouldn't correct that narrative. I completely stopped answering phone calls. Whatever they assumed was the reason I left was certainly more flattering than reality.

Back in Dallas, I rolled my suitcase upstairs and took over my brother's old room. On the bedside table was a gift from my father, which was also an overt suggestion. An NIV Bible and Rick Warren's *The Purpose Driven Life*.

It was time to get right with Jesus.

At first, I struggled to find my footing. All alone in an unfamiliar city. But after a couple of weeks went by, I started to regain my balance. In an effort to build some community and heal, I gravitated to what felt most familiar. I found a Southern Baptist church with a great singles program and poured myself into the ministry. This church now has eight jillion campuses, but at the time, the church was really quite small.

Needless to say, this pastor was incredibly charismatic—you might even say he had a cult following. I couldn't get enough of his no-nonsense sermons. I bought CDs of his previous sermons. This guy was unafraid to deliver a knockout or ruffle the church-goers' feathers. I'm sure that tenacity is exactly why the church has blown up over the last twenty years. I stayed at that church for about a year and a half before becoming a missionary in Thailand (more on that later). After Thailand, it was clear that Jesus had fixed me, and I was able to return to college.

Recently, I was scrolling through TikTok when I spotted a clip of my dear old pastor speaking in his typical handwaving style.

"Deconstruction has become this sort of...sexy thing to do," he said in a mocking tone.

I can't fully explain the sinking sense of betrayal I felt at this fairly short statement. This man was intelligent enough to understand the weight of those words. I had expected that he might have compassion for the hurting, not mock us in the midst of our suffering. Deconstruction—sexy? An existential crisis, *sexy*? I knew in my heart he knew better. In real time I was learning just how painful those famous "knockouts" could feel when you were the recipient. I just never would have imagined that he would punch down for the sake of achieving that end.

I remember the first time I read the word *deconstruction*. I was scrolling through Twitter (I refuse to call it X). In my feed was the late Rachel Held Evans, a *New York Times* best-selling author who boldly challenged the church. A friend had shared a tweet from 2018 in which Rachel wrote, "Healthy deconstruction is like the demolition stage of a remodel—necessary to rebuilding but not the endgame."

I didn't know the word, but I could tell by the context clues that this word was going to be important to me. Giving language for an experience I knew I was having but didn't know how to describe. So I typed "deconstruction" into my Google search bar and was instantly overwhelmed. I learned that there were thousands of us, even hundreds of thousands, who were on this spiritual journey. Truth seekers, like me, who needed some answers for the questions that boiled in our spirits.

We were all so different, attended different churches, experienced different storms...but all of us had experienced, bit by bit, a demolition of faith. Turns out, shared trauma has a way of forging bonds, and in this circle I started forming new friendships. Including one hilarious exvangelical who would eventually become one of my favorite heretics: my dear friend April Ajoy. You see, she'd found that video, was equally appalled, and she made a video of her own out of it.

On TikTok, this kind of video is referred to as a "stitch," as in two videos stitched together. One moment, my former pastor was there on the screen, and then next came a beautiful redhead in a comfy blue sweater, looking baffled and scratching her chin.

"Is deconstruction...sexy?" she asked.

The scene faded into a hilarious montage of April in a fitted red dress, flipping her hair to some bow-chicka-wow-wow and seductively whispering at the camera:

"Was everything I believed a lie? My Christian family's disowned me. My aunt just called me the Antichrist. You know what, though? It was totally worth it. Because deconstruction is soooo sexy."

I didn't know whether to laugh or to cry, but I knew I had found my people. Beneath the humor was an obvious hurt, and it was one that I deeply related to. I smashed "follow" so hard, I about cracked my phone screen. I'd never felt so dang validated.

April is sharp with a ferocious faith, but she's been dealt quite a helping of church hurt. She pulls no punches with her hilarious videos, and she's taken her fair share of licks, too. For every person of faith she validates, there are twenty more she's pissed off. And boy, do they let her know it. I suppose the comments are great for the engagement. The algorithm sure loves outrage. But I also know from personal experience how that hatred can wear on the soul.

These days, when my heretic friends and I share about our faith crises, pastors and fellow believers often tell us the problem lies within ourselves. They suggest that if we had more faith, none of this mess would have happened. Whenever I had a question with no easy answer, I was told to just have faith, lean into the mystery, or simply not ask.

However, my experience—and that of many friends—suggests the opposite: We didn't leave the church because we stopped loving Jesus; we left because we loved Him deeply. Whenever I challenged the rigid, literal interpretations we were taught to accept without question, or the power dynamics that created a culture of abuse, I was made to feel as if my faith was faltering. If I didn't take Scripture literally and submit to church authority, I was seen as an outsider, a dangerous challenge, as if I were an enemy of Jesus.

But we were the ones who watched Him so closely we noticed when a single tile fell. And then another, and then another. When we started to ask questions, we were gaslit and told to have faith. But the tiles kept falling, and before we knew it, Jesus had lost a whole eyeball. Every one of us had tried making patches for years. But the tiles kept falling down. And one day we looked up, and the Jesus we'd loved for so long wasn't there anymore.

We kept looking around us, like "Does nobody else see this?"

And if the church did notice, who knew.

But I can tell you this: It wasn't a lack of faith that sent me running. It was the church's messed-up image of Jesus. I was tired of gaslighting myself.

. . . .

I posted a picture on social media while all this was going on.

It was me, protesting in front of a courthouse, holding a poster that read "JESUS CALLED, HE WANTS HIS RELIGION BACK." And it ruffled more than a few feathers.

NOT THAT WHEEL, JESUS!

I was called a heretic. A wolf in sheep's clothing. A false teacher. A doubting Thomas.

And oddly enough, it was that last one that really stuck to my ribs. The others were so ridiculous and off-base that it was easy to brush them off.

But a doubting Thomas? It is hard to deny. The criticism stung, but it also revealed something deeper—a fear of doubt that runs through so much of the church. I had always been told that doubt was dangerous, that my questions were the enemy of my faith. But the more I read, the more I saw myself in the story of Thomas.

I can vividly recall a sermon from my childhood growing up in Third Baptist Church. It was about THAT guy.

Doubting Thomas.

The one whose name was spit out like an insult.

The one who didn't immediately believe.

I wondered...whatever happened to Thomas? Did Jesus reject him for doubting? Was this loyal disciple condemned? And if so...what did that say about me?

So, I went to the Bible for a little reading, and what did I find?

Y'all, it brought me to tears.

Now Thomas (also known as Didymus), one of the Twelve, was not with the disciples when Jesus came. So the other disciples told him, "We have seen the Lord!"

But he said to them, "Unless I see the nail marks in his hands and put my finger where the nails were, and put my hand into his side, I will not believe."

A week later his disciples were in the house again, and Thomas was with them. Though the doors were locked, Jesus came and stood among them and said, "Peace be with you!" Then he said to Thomas, "Put your finger here; see my hands. Reach out your hand and put it into my side. Stop doubting and believe."

Thomas said to him, "My Lord and my God!"

Then Jesus told him, "Because you have seen me, you have believed; blessed are those who have not seen and yet have believed."   (JOHN 20:24–29)

Sweet, precious Thomas. His questioning made for quite a sermon on the beauty of blind-hearted faith. The thing is, if I had been sitting on the pews of TBC Dothan, the sermon would have ended right there.

Believe.

Don't ask questions. Don't doubt.

Just believe.

But for many of us, that will never be possible. God didn't make us that way. Instead, He gifted us with curious spirits and minds that seek truth and meaning. For years, I tried to suppress the doubt that made my spirit feel itchy. But there is no volume control for questions. They are relentless, insatiable things. Doubt dies only when it finds an answer.

But do you know what I've come to believe?

Doubting Thomas got a really bad rap. The real sin is spiritual certainty.

Jesus had been crucified just days before, and Thomas was grief-stricken and traumatized. All Thomas wanted was to see his Rabbi—like the other eleven disciples. He wasn't dismissing the Resurrection. He was protecting his heart from the incredible devastation of losing Jesus again.

And the most beautiful thing, what we all need to remember, is how Jesus responded to Thomas.

He said, "Here are My wounds. See. Touch. Believe."

He conquered every question. Thomas wasn't rejected for his doubt; instead, he was invited closer. That changed everything for me.

Of course, Jesus added that those who believe without seeing are blessed—and I 100 percent agree. Must be nice to be those guys.

But at this point, I had a Thomas heart. Jesus was my dearest, most precious friend.

Deconstruction, I learned, is not about walking away. It's walking and reaching toward Jesus. Through prayer and tears and reading and wrestling. Through questions that lead to more questions. I didn't walk here. I was led here, and I left with my hand outstretched, reaching toward His wounds. Half anticipating and half terrified, I wanted nothing more than for the wounds to be real and for my faith to return.

Deep down, I knew what was happening.

I wanted to see my Rabbi again. I was hurting and protecting my heart. Doubt didn't signify a lack of faith, but a faith that was thirsting for answers.

God's not afraid of our questions.

Jesus didn't scold our friend Doubting Thomas, and He isn't scolding us either.

I had arrived at a place where I had more questions than answers. My faith had long been punctuated by periods and exclamation points, but this process led me to believe that maybe God was a fan of the question mark.

CHAPTER 6

Homeless Christian

For a couple of months after we left New Hope, I received emails and phone calls from church members who were very...concerned. Concerned for my well-being, my soul, my children. I had more concern than I knew what to do with. Concern coming out of my ears. Not being a complete and total ass, I decided to answer those phone calls. But in the end, the sentiment was always the same.

Can't you forgive and make nice?

As if I were a toddler who'd left church in a tantrum, slamming the door shut behind me. But I wasn't some child who went storming down the hall. And this wasn't my first (or fourth) rodeo. I crawled out of that church holding my insides together. I was internally, spiritually bleeding out. It's a miracle I made it to the parking lot.

This wasn't some boo-boo that I was at home mending.

My relationship with church wasn't gonna be resuscitated by anyone, anytime soon. I practically wrote DNR on my own forehead. Or maybe Do Not Save? DNS? Anyways…leave me alone. Don't bring me back.

I didn't want their concern, their phone calls, or their casseroles. I didn't want to hear another word about "church being a hospital for sinners." If church was indeed a hospital for sinners, it needed its license pulled. Best I could tell, the souls who attended were far sicker than the ones who slept in.

So for the next few Sundays, that's what my family did. We just…slept in. For the kids and Ian, it was like a vacation. For me, it was post-op recovery. I was hurting, quietly nursing my wounds, in shock from the devastating injury.

But as the wounds healed, or at least started to, the quiet in my body took leave. I mean, exit stage left, pursued by a bear. It was followed immediately with anger.

I couldn't get past the injustice of it all. The betrayal. The perpetual abuse. I was pissed, gaining strength, and wanting to fight. Not just my pastor, but the whole institution. I wanted to call it out, the betrayal, the harm, the toxic and dangerous theology. The structure of power that shielded abusers, and then asked victims to "forgive."

You know about the time that Jesus brought a whip to the church and flipped over tables? There's a detail that's frequently overlooked in that story, but it was a detail that didn't escape me. It wasn't a moment of uncontrolled rage that sent Jesus snap-crackle-popping. He had a whole lot of time to think about where He'd be cracking that whip, at whom, and why. Because before Jesus went on that famous rampage, He went home and made the dang whip.

Now, I'm a little vanilla when it comes to these things, but what I do know about whips is this: They're leather and braided, and even in modern times, that process would take a few hours.

Kudos to Jesus, He's the whole standard-bearer. But the truth is, I wasn't going for tables. I was ready to burn the whole thing down.

I had the fuel.

I just needed a match.

And there it was sitting in front of me. A microphone, in my angriest moment.

I mean, I do have a platform of over a million readers. I could…tell them about all of this, couldn't I? I could tell them how harmful the church had been, how they attempted to cover up abuse, how when I reported a deacon for felony crimes, they asked if it was okay that he still use the gym, because "after all, this is a church," right?

Maybe, if I started telling my story, about how religion used me and used me to hurt others, then spit me out like some gristle, maybe then, people would listen.

If a Christian author was saying it?

I turned the idea over in my fingers. It was small, but I could feel its potential. You can't fix a church with a broken foundation. We needed to build it from scratch.

I went nuclear.

Sure, talking about it as a demolition would fit the metaphor a little better. But I was hurt. I was angry. I was angry that I had been hurt and hurt and hurt. I was angry that there was no accountability or consequence for anyone or anything, aside from my spirit. I started cranking out content that reflected the pain I was going through and took aim at the ideas and institutions I held responsible. Anyone new to my feed would have never guessed that it used to be nothing but bubbles and sunshine. Would they have believed that I built my career on inspirational content and videos of me laughing over one of the millions of ways I've managed to embarrass myself in public?

There was an exodus of followers.

"I don't follow you for this."

"Go back to the funny videos, please."

"You're lost."

That number ticking down would usually send me into a panic. This is my livelihood. If I don't have an audience, there is no paycheck. Yes, normally, I would be doing a hard backpedal and overcompensate by going live to cackle about accidentally scaring our mailman on laundry day or something. But this time, it was different.

There's a reason I went with a nuke and not a bulldozer. Bombs do not fit very neatly back into their boxes.

So I watched those numbers tick down with an unfamiliar sense of satisfaction. It feels so damn good to shake the tree sometimes.

Then, a funny thing happened. Those numbers started ticking back up. Brand-new people were finding me. My inbox was becoming less filled with hate mail, and, instead, I was reading messages about finally feeling heard. They were sharing their own stories with me. Stories of how the church they had loved and been dedicated to had harmed them. And they weren't just connecting to my experience. They were hyping me up.

I became the poster girl for deconstruction in some quarters. "GO GET 'EM, MK," they would chant. I was a megaphone for the disenfranchised, the frustrated, the confused, the hurt.

That's the thing about blowing shit up. The resulting atomic cloud looks...incredible. Pillowy and awesome, an eruption that breaks through the atmosphere and can be seen from the satellites. It's beautiful and powerful and churning.

And, heck, with all that bomb cloud, you can't really see the destruction beneath.

For a long time, it simply looks like a wonder, a storm of your own making. I would not stop until the system that hurt me was reduced to a pile of rubble.

And in the postapocalyptic landscape that was my faith when I left the church, I found people like me, walking among the rubble, trying to make sense of the pieces.

And then there were those other people, the ones who were there for the smoke. They would hop into my social feed and scold and tsk-tsk, with zero desire for healing. With every comment and insinuated damnation, they were only affirming my anger. Worse, the people in my community were mostly silent. But their irritation and judgment were palpable. It felt like when your parents give you the look that says they're not angry; they're disappointed.

Not to brag, but I made the cover of *Christianity Today*. Do they even have a cover? Maybe not. Maybe it was just a headline. In some corners of the internet, I topped the list of Christian authors to avoid, and in other corners I was heralded as being a cycle breaker.

It felt like busting out of a mental and spiritual prison, and I was not interested in gatekeeping the hole I had blown into the wall. I made this sort of heretical proselytizing my whole personality and was ready to elevator-pitch it to anyone who would listen. For this middle child who'd been storytelling and performing and longing for attention her whole damn life, it all felt like lifeblood and adrenaline and purpose.

The string that had secured my little balloon to religion was thoroughly cut. Anything a Sunday school teacher had given the side-eye to back in my LifeWay days went straight on the menu of Things MK Must Now Do and Flaunt.

I was high on my freedom and, occasionally, weed. I was reading the work of Rob Bell. I booked an appointment with a fancy sex therapist, and I asked all sorts of questions about my body. (I wish I had some better insights for you from that experience. As it turns out, we're all a little repressed and we all have a little freak in us. Duh.)

I went to a drag show and laughed 'til I cried. I gave money to Planned Parenthood. And when the Supreme Court overturned *Roe v. Wade*, I took to the streets in protest.

It was my heresy era. A Christian Rumspringa. I was a full-blown prodigal child. My split with the church was the kind of breakup where you cut your bangs and hightail it out of town. I was driving as far and as fast as I could, looking for someplace to heal.

I'm not gonna lie, it was a little unhinged. Okay, maybe a lot.

Wherever this faith journey was taking me, I didn't have the slightest clue. I'd asked Jesus to take the whole wheel, and He'd driven me straight off the map.

Even the creepy Facebook algorithm sniffed out the change in my spiritual life. Before long, my news feed was peppered with content from heretics just like me. Actually, that's giving me too much credit. These folks were a hundred times worse. Their names are frequently mentioned in profiles on *Evangelicalism's Most Wanted*.

First, there is Father Nathan Monk, a notorious (former) priest and political provocateur, who initially found fame when he renounced the cloth of the Russian Orthodox Church and stood in support of gay marriage (against Putin, which…let's be honest, is super badass). Believe it or not—I couldn't at first—his story gets wilder from there.

Nathan experienced homelessness as a child (more on that later), and then he turned around and ran multiple shelters. He's been arrested a few times, but all for good trouble. If there's a moment, he's somewhere in it. And not in that he's perpetually drumming in town; he's just…always there when it happens. Sometimes by accident, sometimes by happenstance, but it always makes for a moment.

I genuinely mean it when I say this man's life reminds me of Forrest Gump. No less than three times have I been reading the news and—*boom!*—there's my buddy Nathan. Maybe he's the headline, maybe he's the writer, or maybe in Forrest Gump fashion, he's accidentally hanging out with the president; who knows. It's Nathan. (Go buy his books.)

And then there is April, whom you probably remember. I discovered her while doomscrolling TikTok. She's that quick-witted exvangelical redhead with an affinity for religious black comedy.

April has often been the target of right-wing rage farmers (like Ben Shapiro and Andy Ngo). Still, she never backs down from her message. And her videos make me laugh. Sometimes from shock—she can be pretty spicy—but mostly because she just gets it. The deconstruction, the church hurt, all of it.

April has carried her cross. From the weird, sticky parts of Purity Culture to the disdain of "Christian" politics, to the frequent attacks from other believers who are certain she's going to hell. Perhaps that's the part I relate to most: the perpetual condemnation.

Last year, some soft-boiled egg with a YouTube channel declared me "Heretic of the Week." Devastated, I texted the link to April and asked what she thought I should do about it. She responded with a link, and when I clicked on that video, I damn near wet my britches. April Ajoy was "Heretic of the Year."

Birds of a feather, I guess.

It's wild what happens when you break up with a church. You get stamped with every bad label: false teacher to harlot to heretic to (my personal favorite) "the soulless reincarnate of the fallen Nephilim."

These new friends of mine were routinely getting called all sorts of names, and a lot of those weren't kind. But what blew my mind and filled me with hope was that these "heretic" friends hadn't given up on kindness.

They love the world like Jesus does. They believe that it's all worth saving.

I thank God (and the algorithm) every day that the three of us—Nathan, April, and I—were digitally connected. What started out as friendly online banter between creators in the comment section turned into precious friendship—forged in the fire of cheap shots of whiskey at a karaoke joint in Nashville.

Have you ever heard the joke "A harlot, a priest, and a national best-selling Christian author walk into a bar..."? Okay, it's not really a joke, but it was funny as hell. I keep waiting for the video to emerge. April and I went hard in the paint with some old-school DC Talk, and Nathan danced a little country jig while slaying some Johnny Cash.

We ate trash food (with Prilosec, because this is forty) and stayed up way past our bedtimes. We talked about God, and Christian haunted houses, and how to eat a banana with a fork so the high school guys "wouldn't stumble." There was laughter and tears and even more laughter. And in the hours we spent, and continued to spend, I kept getting the strangest feeling. Something hopeful, yet deeply familiar. Like a memory that hasn't been made. Spending time with these precious friends, it felt...

Like church, but lighter.

Like church, but sweeter.

Like church, but nothing like "church" at all.

· · · · · · · · · ·

As I said earlier, Nathan (the ex-priest and author) experienced homelessness as a child, which is something I struggle to imagine. Yes, my childhood was filled with financial stress and living close to the wire, but we always had a place to come home to. For Nathan, there was no security, no place to lay his head as a kid.

The experience impacted him so profoundly, he dedicated most of his young adult years to running a nonprofit shelter. As you can imagine, that line of work is bound to produce some stories.

But beyond the stories, Nathan challenged me to reconsider my own assumptions about homelessness. During a recent conversation, I gave him a call, wanting his take on what terms I should use in this chapter when referring to the homeless. Should I say homeless? Experiencing homelessness? Unhomed? Unhoused? Off the grid? What would make me sound as compassionate and as up-to-date as possible?

He took a deep breath and rumbled forth with this knowledge drop.

"Look, I get wanting to be sensitive and appropriate and all that. But as someone who grew up this way as a kid, as someone who spent a big chunk of their career working with this population, I don't care what the f*&% you call it, as long as we acknowledge that none of that part of the conversation solves the problem."

Nathan is nothing if not a straight shooter.

As he went on to remind me, for millennia humans were nomadic. The idea of being "home" only if you spent every night inside a human-built structure was not something we as a species assigned parameters to for many centuries. Then, somewhere along the way, we decided to put down roots, stay in one spot, pick out our favorite creek for water and a close-by field for crops, and called it Home Sweet Home.

Now, we've created a whole ideology around the concept of home that has everything to do with buildings and sidewalks, post offices and schools, but that doesn't really speak to what the true heart of home is.

Community.

It broke my heart awhile back when, here in my city, officials took measures to clean up a homeless encampment. Those who weren't living in traditional houses, who weren't living traditional lifestyles, had moved into a park and had developed their own little municipality.

There was a garden that everyone tended. People helped take care of each other's children so they could go work jobs and look for resources. And when the city came in to reclaim the park property and clear things out, what that group lost was their community.

I'm not trying to claim that situations like this one are the rule and not the exception. There were also instances of drug abuse and domestic violence and all manner of crimes and misdemeanors at Tent City.

But guess what? You and I both know that even though we live in our tidy houses, along tidy sidewalks, with our tidy mailboxes, we ourselves have neighbors who are addicts, who are violent, who commit crimes. It just feels more familiar and containerized and "normal," the way we "housed" people do it.

Nathan reminded me that we've got a weird way of determining who we see as "homeless." Since when did committing to a piece of property make you more of a person? Did it signal that home was a priority for you? And lest we all get too big in our own britches, he further reminded me of the sobering stat that 80 percent of us in the States, E I G H T Y P E R C E NT, are one paycheck away from destitution.

Why do I bring all this up?

I'd always correlated the validity of my faith journey with how regularly I met in a building with other like-minded people. And here I was, hanging out in a whiskey bar with Nathan and April, no pew to my name anymore, feeling like I was home. Spiritually fed. Loved, even.

I'd had well-meaning church folks reach out to me throughout that time. They were worried that I had "left the church," that I was wandering aimlessly in a savage world, danger at every curve. They fretted that I was open to the elements. And to be honest, based on the way I'd always thought about church and here-is-the-church-and-here-is-the-steeple, they weren't wrong. In the sense in which we'd collectively defined it, I was homeless.

But.

I was learning so much out here, sleeping under the stars. I kept thinking about Abraham, asking big questions of God, about why things were the way they were and when things were supposed to work out and how all this thing called life runs. God told Abraham to get his butt outside and to look up, to quit making the ceiling of his understanding of God just the inside roof of his tent.

It was when Abraham got out of his house and stared into the sky that he began to really see the promises of God.

CHAPTER 7

Catfish

I don't know what it is about holidays in my family, but we can't get through a single one without some sort of ridiculous spectacle. It was Easter Sunday 2019, and the Backstroms were celebrating in our typical catastrophic fashion. The whole mess started the week before, when I snuggled up with my children on the couch to discuss the meaning of Easter.

Naturally, the kids had quite a few questions.

Did Jesus grow wings? What happened to gravity? Isn't the air hard to breathe way up high? Wouldn't it be funny if He was flying like Superman? Where does the bunny come in?

When my best efforts were finally exhausted, both kids seemed pretty excited about the resurrection of Jesus. And I ain't gonna lie, my little Protestant heart went pitter-pat over what a great job I had done.

I am such a good mother, I thought to myself, tucking them into bed. Ian prepared their Easter baskets, and then we both fell asleep.

At 3:00 am, a bloodcurdling screech.

"MOMMY—HE'S HERE! HELP ME, MOMMY!"

I ran to Ben's bedroom, where he was sitting straight up with terror.

"There's nobody here, baby. Are you okay? What's wrong?"

"I saw HIM," Ben whispered, looking me dead in the eye like some child from a horror movie.

"Who?" I asked.

He leaned in and whispered, "The ghost of the risen Christ."

GREAT.

So, that went on for an hour or more. After checking closets and under the bed for Zombie Jesus, I started to wonder if maybe some Bible stories might not be suitable for imaginative children. Or at least not the ones prone to night terrors. Or kids with the last name "Backstrom."

Eventually, everyone went back to sleep and Easter morning arrived. Baskets were opened, adorable outfits donned, and the children burst outside with candy-fueled energy to enjoy the sunshine of spring.

And then, another bloodcurdling scream.

"MOMMMMMMY! MOMMY! HELP! COME QUICK!"

I sprinted down the hall, figuring if Jesus was making an appearance in broad daylight, I should be there to say hi.

But stepping out onto our front porch, it looked like I'd entered a crime scene. The kids were sobbing and pointing under the bench. I leaned down to get a good look. Amid the blood, the fur, and the chaos, I spotted one furry victim.

"Waffles KILLED the Easter Bunny!" Holland wailed in horror.

I was dumbfounded. I couldn't find words. Our cat isn't the most prolific hunter, but when he does bring a "present," it's usually a tiny mole or a field mouse. Nothing super...substantial.

But this: a bunny. On Easter morning. What were the freaking chances?

So, I'm on my hands and knees in my Sunday best, dry-heaving with a handful of paper towels, trying to scoop Easter Bunny guts into a grocery bag.

This is fine, this is fine, this is fine.

It was 100 percent not fine.

I tried convincing my sobbing children that this wasn't the actual Easter Bunny. That he's probably white or colorful like an Easter egg. But I'd recently admitted that I'd never seen him. So they weren't buying it, and that's fair.

Then my son, the imaginative one, tells his sister not to worry.

"It's Easter, Holland. It's gonna be okay! Jesus can just resurrect him!"

With visions of *Pet Sematary* swirling in my head, I couldn't help but wonder if maybe these conversations with my children about Jesus were getting a bit lost in translation.

· · · · · · · · ·

The first funeral I remember experiencing was that of my great-grandmother Beatrice. There were plenty of other funerals I attended before hers, but none where I truly mourned. With Bea, I was finally old enough to experience grief—to feel acutely the immense loss of everything she was.

And my God, was her presence beautiful in my life. When I hear her name, the memories that rush in are so colorful, and so real, it is jarring.

Decades have passed since I last walked through her door, and yet if I close my eyes…and knock, I can see her smile through the glass storm door, delighted at an unannounced visit. I can feel my knees pressing into the soft green carpet that filled the front room of her tiny brick rancher. There's a dainty blue chair in front of the TV, from which she would shoo away my parents, insisting she could manage the grandbabies alone.

"I haven't killed one yet," she would laugh. And they'd leave us to watch CBS.

I spent hours on that carpet, sitting crisscross applesauce in front of the box TV, watching *The Andy Griffith Show* and eating little teacups of Breyers Vanilla Bean Ice Cream. Sometimes, we'd pull out the massive collection of crystal glass piggy banks, dump all the coins on that green carpet, and sort through the change for hours.

As time slipped, we'd follow the sun's warmth to the other side of the house through the quaint galley kitchen and over to the floral couch in a room full of windows. We'd pore over all Bea's photo albums, laughing and telling stories, until one of our bellies growled.

Then she'd throw burgers on in the cast-iron skillet, and like clockwork, when they were just about ready, there'd be a tiny little knock at the sunroom door.

And in would walk her next-door neighbor, Bob Bob.

Bob Bob was a tiny old man who lived in his overalls tending a little snap pea garden. He was always humming, and he had quite a nose for my great-grandmother's famous burgers.

"Oh, am I interrupting you?" he'd ask, fiddling with his overalls. "I was just coming to ask about all those ferns—but looks like you're about to eat dinner!"

"Bob Bob, you knew damn well that you smelled these burgers," Bea would say with a chuckle while fixing him a plate. But she was always glad to take his bait, because if there was one thing she loved more than feeding old Bob Bob, it was getting attention for her pet ferns.

Those plants were her pride and joy—and the envy of every old lady in Mayfair. And about once a day some Patsy or June would compliment my great-grandmother's ferns, asking how they got so big, and how she kept them in the winter. Bea would answer in meticulous detail about how she managed this magic.

Spray bottles, not watering cans. Warm water, not cold. A little bit of coffee grounds occasionally mixed into the soil. A little this, a little that, and a whole lot of love, she would say.

And those fern-jealous women would scribble down notes like some murder trial court reporters. But whether or not they took Bea's advice, it was hard to know. Because while Bea's ferns were as lively and lush as the Amazon, her neighbors' ferns never got any bigger.

A couple of years before Beatrice died, I popped into her house for a visit. As I was finishing my teacup of ice cream, she asked if I'd help run an errand.

"Lowe's just got a new batch of ferns," she said. "And I hear they're even bigger than mine. Can we do a quick drive-by? Check things out?"

"Sure," I said, raising an eyebrow. "But we're just driving and looking, right?"

"Well, let's take your car, just in case," she replied. "The trunk's a little bit bigger."

Bea was right: Those puppies were monstrous. You could see them from across the whole parking lot.

"Slow down," she whispered as we approached the nursery. Her eyes narrowed as if looking for something. She crossed her arms and frowned.

"God dammit, they're bigger than mine."

"Bea!" I exclaimed, my eyes open wide—half from the shock of hearing her say it, and half from utter delight.

"Oh, act like you've heard a cussword before. And pull into that spot over there."

No sooner had I put my vehicle in park than my great-grandmother pulled out a wad of twenties and placed them in the palm of my hand.

"Those three ferns, right there on the curb," she said, pointing back at the nursery. "Go get them for me, will you? And if anyone sees you making the purchase, don't tell them that I'm in the car."

Beatrice looked back and forth as if she were scouting the area for cops. Suddenly, this sweet little errand with Granny was feeling a whole lot more like a drug deal.

I got out of the car and looked back at my great-grandmother, who was now shielding her face with a magazine. Not from the sun, I was realizing. But from the eyeballs of potential witnesses.

And that was the day that I found out Beatrice didn't actually have a green thumb, and neither did she have a meticulous care plan for those ferns. What she did have was a friend named Bill who worked in the nursery at Lowe's and tipped her off every season when the best of the ferns came in.

I've never laughed as hard as I did that afternoon, dragging Bea's trash cans into the garage so she could discreetly get rid of the old ferns. Then we swept her front porch, and I ran to the car while she made sure no one was watching, and we filled up her pots with the biggest damn ferns that Mayfair had ever seen.

The morning of the funeral, I wore pearls. I'd called Momma on speakerphone while I was getting ready, and she'd explained that pearls, not diamonds or anything flashy, were appropriate to wear at a funeral. I don't know which part of that made me mad, but it did. So I asked which stupid asshole wrote the rule book on what you're supposed to wear when you're sad that somebody died. Not that I had diamonds or cared either way. It just seemed like a stupid rule.

"I'm sad too," was all she replied before the line went silent. I realized I was being horrible, but that didn't give me a filter. Maybe this is what they mean about the first stage of grief. You're just angry. Angry about everything. Anger at the loss, at the person you lost; anger at God for making you love them; anger at God for taking them away. Anger at dead people and living people and God and everybody. Anger at the stupid asshole who made rules about wearing diamonds to a funeral.

I apologized to Momma and she told me it was unnecessary. I hung up the phone and stepped back from the mirror.

Eyes swollen, neck splotchy and red, I looked as wretched as I felt. I'd skipped over makeup completely, deciding that any effort on my part to appear unshattered was going to be a fruitless one. I sucked in my stomach and tugged at the sides of my dress, whispering one more curse against the supposed rules for funeral attire. Buttons and zippers shouldn't be required when you're all hunkered over from grief.

I decided that as soon as the funeral was over, I was gonna call my best friend and request a couple of promises. *If I die before you, please make sure my funeral doesn't suck. Tell everyone to wear comfy pajamas. Play happy music. Serve cheese dip and weed brownies; it'll be hilarious.* And they'd roll their eyes and promise to do it, when we both knew the truth was: They'd never.

Because everyone follows the funeral rule book. We'll break promises but never etiquette. My grandmother's pearls are a broken promise. So is this stupid black dress. When I was thirteen years old, Bea made me promise to sing a song at her funeral. When I agreed, she cackled with glee.

"Good, now let me tell you which song."

That was quite the phone call to make.

"Hey, Dad. I know you're in charge of planning the funeral—and here's the thing: Bea made me promise I'd sing a song at her funeral and wear a red sequined dress. What song? Well, that's actually the weird part."

The family was escorted to the front of the church, where Bea's casket lay covered in flowers. The pastor was making his way to the pulpit, and a full choir was seated behind him. I dabbed away tears and picked up the program. Some Scripture, some stories, some traditional hymns, wrapped up with a tidy benediction. It was all going to be so beautifully boring.

I imagined what would happen if I walked up onstage and interrupted that nice Presbyterian pastor.

"Ladies and gentlemen, as many of you know, our beloved Bea had a wicked sense of humor." I'd grab the mic off the pulpit. A jazz band would roar to life behind me, and to the horror of everyone, I'd sing: "I'll Be Glad When You're Dead, You Rascal You."

I'd love to report that that's how we did it. But that's not how it went down. Not by a long shot.

We did all the proper things. There were a couple of sedate hymns. The pastor took to the pulpit, giving a message about the nice Christian lady things Bea had done. There were a couple of attempts at levity about her run of bad luck at bingo. There was a recitation about her dependability as a volunteer. She got packaged up in tidy little rectangular paragraphs.

Pew-sitter, casserole-giver, nice old lady kinda crap. Nothing like the woman I knew.

But here's the thing. All around me during Bea's funeral, people across the church auditorium chuckled at the right places, sniffled at the right places, and nodded their heads at all the right things.

Gone was her color. Gone was her vibrancy.

Gone was her spitfire humor.

How could all these people, who lived life beside Bea, who sat beside her at bingo and heard her sailor's mouth, sit here in quiet complicity?

Sitting in the church that day, I felt myself start to dissociate. Perhaps I was trying to escape my anger, my confusion, over how this played out. We'd all shown up to this family affair, and we were all crying very real tears, but I couldn't shake this lingering suspicion that some of us were at the wrong funeral.

It was like we didn't know the same person at all.

You know what I'm starting to believe?

Church is a funeral.

We get together and remember this guy that we all claim to know, who died under tragic circumstances. We re-create His last meal that He had with His besties. We talk about when He died and how He died and why His death should matter.

But here's the thing. We don't talk so much about His rabble-rousing. We don't like to get too in the weeds with His activism, with His insistence on elevating the downtrodden. We might give an occasional mention of how He shook up the religious establishment, but we don't want to go too far down the rabbit hole lest we end up flipping our own tables.

That Jesus was too spicy, I suppose, for the elders. So they made up a flavorless Christ. As pale and stale as a Communion cracker. But the church kept choking it down.

Yep, that's our guy; we'd all nod our heads. All in the name of unity.

It worked for me, until it didn't.

Until I ran into hard questions—questions that reminded me of the same feeling I had sitting in that church at Bea's funeral. The same sanitized stories. The same stripped-down version of someone who was so much more complex, bold, and subversive.

It made me realize that the way we tell stories about people isn't just shaped by how we see them, but also by how we think the audience will perceive them. We might adjust the narrative to reach them—but even then, what's heard can be very different from what's said. The gap between truth and perception can be surprisingly wide.

Maybe it's just human nature—this need to connect, to be understood—that leads us to shape the truth in ways we think will resonate. We smooth the edges, adjust the tone, in the hope that it'll bring us closer to others. But in doing so, the essence of what we're trying to convey can sometimes get lost in translation.

Like when my friend John, a pastor from Maryland, had a middle school assembly go sideways in Alabama. Poor John. He'd planned to talk to the kids about Jesus—the spicy version. The guy who flipped tables, made His own whip, and would probably have jazz at His funeral. John was so excited to share this message, pouring his heart into it, until he realized in real time that things had gone completely off the rails. I can't help but laugh imagining him, standing in a sea of middle schoolers, wondering what went wrong to make them go blink, blink, blink.

A little context: John was raised in Maryland. He didn't grow up in the South. Our churchified culture and deep-fried neuroses were all very foreign to him. He did spend a few years in Florida after seminary, but I don't think that helped him acclimate. A map might say that Florida is southern, but every Southerner will tell you: It isn't.

Travel along the panhandle of Florida, and you'll notice the culture shift. Somewhere between the palm trees and the pines, people start frying their vegetables. The orange groves melt into peanut farms and the stripper billboards disappear, replaced with billboards for church. And next thing you know, all the radio stations are either country or contemporary Christian.

That's how you know you're in the uppercase S South. The default settings are different. There's sugar in our tea, there's prayer in our schools, and our Jesus supports open carry.

Which brings us back to my buddy John—who'd just moved to Alabama when he was invited to speak at a local middle school by the president of First Priority, a student-led Christian club. He poured his whole heart into planning that talk, even splurging on full-color, poster-sized pictures of Jesus from all over the world. John hoped to show the "many faces of Jesus," both literally and figuratively. Then he'd ask the students to describe their Jesus, and how He compared with the others. It was a two birds/one stone approach. Challenge cultural norms, encourage critical thinking, give the students a little something to chew on.

As the kids filed into the middle school gym, John placed the posters on an easel. The student president led the assembly in prayer and then introduced John as guest speaker.

"Who is Jesus?" John asked the room, walking over to the stack of posters.

"My Savior!" the president proudly declared.

"A King!" another student responded.

"The Son of God!" yelled a girl in the front row.

All the expected Sunday school answers.

John smiled. "Yes, those are all great answers. But I still want to know…who is Jesus?"

John flipped the first illustration around, revealing Nigerian Jesus. A Black, bearded man with dreadlocks and sandals. A crown of thorns lay on His head.

"Is this Jesus?" John asked the kids. A few shook their heads in response.

He pulled another poster. This time, Chinese.

"Is this Jesus?" he asked again.

John shared each poster, one at a time, and continued repeating the question. And poster by poster, he couldn't help but notice the silence in the room growing thick. Finally, he revealed an American illustration of Jesus with flowing blond hair. There was a flicker of recognition in the eyes of the students. A few seemed to sigh with relief.

"Is this Jesus?" John asked the students, and the resounding answer was yes.

He could've stopped there, and I bet if he had, the sermon would've been a hit. But the lesson plan called for one more photo…and this one didn't come from a church. It was a forensic reconstruction created by archaeologists. The most accurate depiction of Christ. John flipped over the final picture, revealing a dark-skinned, Middle Eastern Jewish man.

"Actually, kids…what if I told you that Jesus wasn't white?"

The students sat quietly, blinking in the bleachers, stunned by this new information.

Sometimes I think about how funny it is that American Jesus is some sort of chameleon. Throw darts at a map and you'll hit multiple variants of Christ. If one hits anywhere in the vast part of the board known as Texas, Jesus' tears are specially reserved for unborn babies and capital gains taxes. Aim up and to the right and Jesus calls on His followers to house immigrants and get out the vote. If the wind blows south with a hard left, you land on Kanye West. Don't ask me why.

Stay with me now, but sometimes I think about that scene in *Talladega Nights* where Ricky Bobby is saying grace with his family. He insists on praying to Eight-Pound, Six-Ounce, Newborn Infant Jesus because he likes the baby version best. His son likes to imagine Jesus is a ninja, and his best friend thinks of Jesus wearing a tuxedo shirt. It's a hilarious commentary on how we've wound up with so many different versions of Jesus.

Easter Zombie Jesus. Tuxedo T-Shirt Jesus, who wants to be formal but is here to party, too. We've got more Jesuses than we know what to do with and collect them like Pokémon. And in trying to find our favorite Jesus, somewhere along the way, we've lost Him.

We've lost Jesus.

I think I know what those middle schoolers were feeling when confronted with a potentially accurate rendering of their personal Lord and Savior. It's more than a little jarring to feel catfished by a Jesus 1.0. That experience has been derailing for me as a grown-up. I can only imagine what they thought:

If the final poster of Jesus was real, then who the heck is that sparkly-eyed white guy on Nana's wall? What are you gonna tell me next, that Jesus was actually named Joshua? Better yet, who the heck is this John guy, anyway, and why is he changing Jesus?

The kids all blink, blink, blinking at John carried their own picture of Jesus. I imagine it had a lot in common with the picture I carried with me. A mix-and-match combo of the many Jesuses we've encountered along the way. A new Jesus, curated from the pieces we decided to keep—the ones that fit our values and made us feel good about ourselves.

My Jesus was a Republican, until He wasn't.

My Jesus was a Democrat, until He wasn't.

He was white, until He wasn't.

He was angry, until He wasn't.

He was Baptist, Presbyterian, Methodist, until He wasn't.

Or maybe…until I wasn't?

It's wild how I always managed to worship a Jesus who looked and thought like me. The portrait of Jesus I carried with me became smudged from the constant erasure.

If the Jesus I've always known was a reflection of my own beliefs, my culture, my upbringing, then who is He really? Who is the Jesus that doesn't fit neatly into the boxes I've created?

I wanted to know Him—the real Him.

Because I now realized that all those years, I hadn't been chasing the image of God.

All along, I had been remaking God in my image.

CHAPTER 8

Evolution

When I was in high school, there was this little store called LifeWay Christian that was hotter than a youth group romance. If you wanted the newest color of a WWJD bracelet, this was the place to be. My favorite was the limited-edition rainbow bracelet. It sold out in a day, but my boyfriend and I snagged up the last two. I wore that bracelet every single day until the Lord told that boy to break up with me. Then I threw it away and replaced it with a black one because I am nothing if not a tad dramatic.

LifeWay had a hold on me that's hard to explain. There was a serious section for grown-ups where men could buy Bibles and books by Joel Osteen, and ladies could pick up some Amish romance novels. But the other side of the store was like Spencer's for saved people. With ironic T-shirts, VeggieTales socks, and CDs by DC Talk, I could spend hours there reading stories about martyrs, checking out cloth Bible covers, and snooping on couples in the relationship section who were trying their best to "kiss dating goodbye," but doing a terrible job.

And let's not forget about Christian bumper stickers—Jesus Is My Co-Pilot; Got Jesus?; and the cowboy kneeling by the cross. All classic choices for the run-of-the-mill Christ Follower, but that's not what I was. I was a warrior, a provocateur, a woman on a holy mission. Which meant the sticker on my car needed to make a statement. For God. Against culture. With pizzazz. So I went with the holographic picture of the Christian fish with its mouth open wide, eating the symbol for evolution. Let's just say that my love affair with science didn't start until a little bit later.

This was the early 2000s when the culture wars were getting cranked up. The fish sticker business was serious, folks. The first generation was just a plain fish, but then some God-hating satanists (probably) responded with a version that had sprouted legs. They put this sticker on the back of their Hondas and ironically drove them around our little town like a mobile billboard for blasphemy. To a seventeen-year-old Baptist youth group kid, it felt like watching somebody slap God. And God just took it, which I didn't understand. But in the end, I prayed the Prayer of Jabez for God to expand my territory and found that shiny fish sticker, with its evolution-chomping mouth, like it was an answer to prayer. I slapped that little puppy on my car and drove out into the mission field.

Now, if I'm being honest with myself, I likely leaned so hard into what felt like such an in-your-face bumper sticker because I wanted to make sure everyone around me knew I was loudly and proudly one of God's children. Deep down, I was compensating for the shame I felt every time I was scolded for asking questions about God. My need to understand was always classified as doubt, not curiosity. I was bad.

And so I wanted there to be no doubt in anyone's mind—not even a stranger stuck behind me in a Taco Bell drive-thru—that I was a good Christian. How could God love me if I was bad? Doesn't He want His children to obey and follow His Word to the letter? I imagined God as one of those parents who gave a terse "Because I said so," to questions, exasperated with a child who won't just do what they're told for once so He can enjoy His morning coffee while it's still hot.

Back then, I thought God was just some grouchy chair-sitter who was perpetually pissed off by my questions and missteps. But now, in the middle of my deconstruction journey, as I was busy burning it all down, I couldn't help but wonder if I had gotten God wrong. What if He wasn't upset at my questions? What if He was actually the standard-bearer of patience and grace? If I, in all my brokenness, can look at my children with overwhelming love, delighting in their curiosity and growth, then how much more must God feel that way about us? What if He's not actually watching us with frustrated disappointment as we fumble along the way? What if He's proud of our desire to grow, to understand, and even evolve? It's a radical thought, but one that changes everything about how we approach our faith and our failures.

It's kinda like that marshmallow experiment I saw on Tik-Tok a little while back. It was an experiment in delayed gratification. Back in the 1970s, some very smart folks at Stanford decided to test how delayed gratification is understood in children, and at what age the ability to show self-restraint begins to show up. Every so often, a late-night host or show about kids saying the darnedest things re-creates the experiment on camera and millions of viewers tune in. Nowadays, the marshmallow experiment makes pretty frequent rounds on social media. Not because we as a society have an intellectual interest in what the experiment reveals about its subjects, but because the subjects are so stinking cute.

The whole thing starts with a camera focused on a table and a chair in a room. Sitting in that chair is a Squishmallow human whose cuteness cannot be contained. I'm telling you, every kid in the study videos is the most darling thing you've ever seen. It makes me wonder if that was the single threshold for signing up.

Needed: Absolutely darling children with wide, expressive eyes. Must love sugar. Call us for an important study. But first, ask your parents.

Each segment of the video begins with said darling child, unaware they are being filmed, sitting in the chair at the table with a single marshmallow on a plate. The study leader walks in and informs the child in very simple terms that if they sit alone in this room and leave the current marshmallow be for one minute, then they'll get another marshmallow. They'll double their marshmallow investment in sixty seconds. The only rule is they can't eat the one on the table yet.

The study leader then leaves the room, the camera keeps rolling…and shit gets hilarious.

I probably don't have to explain how funny it is to watch children squirming in their seats, suffering in silence, completely and utterly soul-deep tortured by the presence of a single marshmallow. But I relate to it on a visceral level. I see that discomfort, and I just…understand it.

I was so tickled by this study, and the viral videos that it created, that I decided to run this exact experiment on my two children. Ben was first, my oldest and most boisterous child. He was about five when we ran this experiment, and it went pretty much exactly as expected. He sat down. I gave him a Little Debbie brownie because my kids didn't really like marshmallows, and I walked away with the camera hidden in plain sight. As one does.

Except, Ben is the child of a millennial. He knew there was a camera around somewhere. He spotted it, popped the brownie into his mouth, and started dancing around like this was a show. It was funny, but it taught me absolutely nothing. A small child not having a shred of impulse control is news to no one.

So I moved on to our second subject. I was hopeful with my daughter, Holland, that she might defy the odds and show herself to be one of those unicorn children who do as they're told, even with a lump of sugary dopamine beckoning her like Carol Anne to a snowy television.

Holland was adorable in her little Elsa pajamas, her hair still a bird's nest from the night before. She sat on a chair in front of the brownie. I explained the rules, that if she waited, she would get another treat. I saw a flicker of light in her eyes, and then I walked away.

And what I learned that day, well, it was not what I expected. I was hoping for some adorable footage of a twisted-up mouth, eyes that looked longingly like a puppy seeing bacon, maybe a whimper or a squirm in the chair.

But what I did not expect to see was my daughter skillfully carving herself a large slice of chocolaty goodness from the middle of the brownie, popping it into her mouth, looking around the room, and then pressing the brownie back together.

She did this with the skill of a Beverly Hills plastic surgeon closing up a tummy tuck, y'all. She was committed to the illusion, as if the bite never happened. Mind you, she was approximately two years old at the time. I watched this footage with horror.

Oh my God, I've created a monster.

Maybe it was all those crime documentaries I watched when she was a baby. She could have learned it by osmosis. Perhaps it's genetic or something. I thought back to all the times that I did similarly tricky and terrible things, and then my feeling of dread only deepened. To my abject horror (and utter amusement), I'd created one just like me.

She was bad...and delightfully so.

I get the impression that a lot of Christians on this planet think that God is looking down on His children as if He's watching in horror at some kind of marshmallow experiment gone bad. As if He sees us down here, pushing two halves of a brownie back together, like "Oh no, I've created a monster!"

Sorry to disappoint you folks, but I don't believe that God's been taken off guard. In my heart, I know that He isn't surprised or disappointed in the least. A father is delighted in all of his children, from their heads to their wiggly toes. Including their expected imperfections. We are human, after all.

As a parent, sure, I was mildly concerned by my daughter's little brownie work-around, much more than my son's joyful shirking of the rules. But I was also delighted by her impish, creative brain. I was both. One hundred percent both. How much more should our heavenly Father adore the ones He created? He certainly gets more of a hand in the process than I did when making my two. And still, I adore them. Including their messes.

Because that's what good parents do.

When Ian and I found out we were having a daughter, he was so excited. We already had a little boy who went through life like Wreck-It Ralph. So, I figured that what he was expecting from Holland was some softness to balance it out.

"Hey," I said, waddling into the kitchen eight months pregnant. "I don't know what you are expecting…but none of the girls in my family fit the whole 'sugar and spice' criteria."

"You know what," Ian laughed, taking a sip of his coffee, "I don't care if she's sweet or whatever. Actually, I hope she's, like, really…bad. Spicy and sassy and dramatic. Ya know?"

I gaped at him for a moment.

But then, it caught. And I knew he was right.

Yes! A girl born wild, hardwired to stand up to people and to challenge the obstacles ahead. Less sugar and spice. More fire and life.

I loved it. I wanted it, too.

And boy did we get what we prayed for.

Holland is every bit all of those things and then some. She entered the world like a wrecking ball and has been making a mark ever since. She's a bona fide brownie surgeon, a raucous comedian, and has a bleeding heart for all of God's creatures…most especially dying rodents. I've become good friends with the local wildlife rehab guy. We have an ongoing text thread of pictures.

"Will this baby squirrel make it?"

"Sure, bring it in."

"What about this one."

"He's gone to see Jesus."

Yes, it can be exhausting at times, raising a wildling who loves to save wild things. But I wouldn't want Holland to be any other way. She's a sour patch kid, and I love her.

What I didn't realize in my LifeWay days was that God might feel the same way about me. His wildling child. His sour patch daughter. The one who asks all the weird questions in church. The one who breaks all the rules. For the longest time, I just figured He viewed me as some sort of failed marshmallow experiment. Some accidental variation of the original recipe.

After all, Sunday school had taught me that brokenness wasn't just part of me—it *was* me. Thanks to Eve, I was fundamentally flawed, and the only way to be worthy of love was to suppress the wildness, erase the questions, and follow the rules I could never seem to keep.

But it was too late, and I was sent to earth this way. A curse on my whole entire family. To be sure, we're all loud and obstinate women. So there's only one explanation. Either God got busy with a bunch of other stuff, or we were stamped out of a really bad batch (and I don't know about you, but to me that sounds a bit ridiculous).

Or, hear me out…maybe He made us this way on purpose. Curious, sweet-and-sour creations. God's own little sour patch kids.

Maybe our wild and unruly natures are less of a bug and more of a feature.

I wish I could go back and hug that girl with her unimpeachable righteousness plastered along her bumper. I would squeeze her tight and tell her that she isn't bad, not by a long shot. That in God's eyes, she is loved. From her head to her toes (even wearing that adorable teal bathing suit). I don't know if she'd be in a place to believe it, but I'd want her to at least hear it. The poor thing would likely be horrified by the knowledge that, like that godless quadrupedal fish, she would also evolve.

Years after I graduated, but before I began growing into a version of myself that would surely give the high school me a brutal IBS flare-up, I watched what has now become one of my favorite episodes of television, ever. It was from a quirky sitcom called *My Name Is Earl*. It's about a guy named Earl (bet you figured that part out) who wins the lottery. A lot of other stuff happens, but the basic premise is that Earl uses his newfound wealth to do good in the world, not because he cares all that much, but because of karma. The show was lighthearted and comical, a refreshing palate cleanser between the murder shows that have strangely become every woman's comfort genre.

My favorite character by a mile was Joy, the titular Earl's ex–partner in crime. She's a hot, Southern mess, brimming with charm and constantly creating chaos. (Relatable.)

While the main plot of my aforementioned favorite episode was forgettable (it was something about a car sale gone wrong), it's the subplot involving a diamond necklace that Joy is just desperate to own that tickles me still. If you've watched any television in the last twenty years, you know the necklace.

No, seriously, you do.

Jane Seymour did a collaboration with Kay Jewelers, and you couldn't watch a half hour of network TV without seeing a commercial for her Open Hearts necklace. Now, I don't vividly remember this necklace because of the millions of ads, or the novelty of Dr. Quinn, Medicine Woman, promoting some cheap strip mall jewelry.

I remember that necklace because it was made of two connected and open heart shapes...which looked like two connected butts. I can still hear my friends cackling over the "booty butt" necklace during *American Idol* commercial breaks. And not to deflate your hope for society, but every one of us is now raising children.

The product placement was strong with this one and Joy was the target demographic. She becomes obsessed with the damn thing, which she cannot afford, but probably could if Earl gave her some of that lottery karma cash that he won in the very first episode. Since that isn't happening, she settles for the logical next option: signing up for a science fair to disprove evolution and collect some prize money. Five hundred dollars would be enough for the necklace and a hot date at the Golden Corral. So Joy gets to planning, and it's that bit—her so-called "science experiment"—that wins every laugh in the episode.

Joy has a particular appeal to me, as I have always had a soft spot for villains. I'd describe her to you, but her character did that best with this iconic television debut:

"You know the kind of woman who could've been the next Faith Hill, but somewhere along the way discovered peach daiquiri, put a diaphragm in on her own, and wound up smack dab in the middle of trailer hell raising two kids? Yep, she still manages to look hot and you can bounce a quarter off her butt cause you gotta take care of yourself. I mean, come on. Anyway, that's me. My name is Joy."

The trailer park Jackie Onassis, y'all. Truly, an American treasure.

Like many Southern women I know and love, Joy is a very devout Christian. Sure, she is also a chain-smoking con artist, but that never stopped anyone from loving the Lord. Joy plans to win this children's science fair not just for that necklace, but to deliver a win for God.

And with that ambitious goal as her carrot, Joy starts sciencing. She creates a little ecosystem for her fish and places the only food on top of a rock. She then adds a fish from a pond, giving it an opportunity to sprout legs or, rather, not sprout legs and then die of starvation and prove evolution is a bunch of bullcrap. However, this plan doesn't go as expected, because wouldn't you know it...the fish goes ahead and grows a pair of legs, right before Jesus and everybody.

Joy is devastated (and confused) by this outcome, and she dives straight into a spiritual tailspin.

If evolution is real, what does that mean about God? What else has she been lied to about? Where does this tower-of-faith Jenga collapse?

Thank goodness for Joy, a friend shows up to explain that the fish was actually a tadpole, which just so happened to be designed by God to "evolve" into a frog.

I know Joy. I mean, not really; she's a character on a show. More accurately, what I do know of Joy is the journey she takes (and all right, a little of the accent). I know what it's like for my big God Experiment to crash and leave everyone gawking. I know what it's like to perceive something as a glitch when it turns out to be a feature of God's design.

And maybe I know a little of that tadpole, too. Of its instinctive, adaptive survival. I realized that my faith was going to have to crawl out of the water and sprout some legs if it was gonna survive.

And that's not a failure—that's the whole point.

CHAPTER 9

The Perfect House

It was nice out there, living beneath the stars, surrounded by heretic friends.

Away from the church. Away from the steeple. Away from the judgment of all its people. No Hell Houses, or purity rings, or bathing-suit checks. No theology too dangerous to challenge.

It was like I'd discovered this brave new world, with less trauma and much longer weekends. When we were living in Florida, it was fairly easy to go about our churchless business. At least there, fewer people asked about what I believed or which church I attended. Honestly, the cultural apathy toward church gave me a moment of reprieve just to process.

Then, we moved back to Sweet Home Alabama (land of a billion churches). Ian started a new job, the kids started a new school, and that typically would've been the moment I'd start the search for our new church home.

Except this time, I didn't.

It wasn't even on my radar.

Perhaps I was a homeless Christian, but I was content in my little tent city. I saw no reason to change. And so time kept flying, and before I knew it, a whole year of Sundays had flown.

None of us had cast a shadow on the door of a church. And to be honest, I wasn't missing it at all. And if the kids missed it, they didn't say so. I don't know many kids eager to put on scratchy clothes and sit on a pew for an hour when they could be watching cartoons and running wild.

But, now I was in the capital S South. Alabamians will ask you where you go to church as casually as asking about the weather.

At least five times a week, I'd get questioned about where my children and I were planning to attend. By relatives, pool friends, strangers at the grocery store. And if I wasn't asked, my children were. They were invited to VBS, Bible study, all the things. Half the sports teams were sponsored by churches.

It was kinda hard to escape church culture, and I was surprised at how much it annoyed me.

Did I used to do this?

Evangelize constantly?

Of course, the answer was YES.

I'd been the most overeager offender. I was one inch away from carrying a karaoke machine to the Walmart parking lot.

I wasn't just a churchgoer. I was a church recruiter. I'd been a worship leader, a campus minister, a missionary. Even now, I'm a Christian author.

But what I'd never before experienced was being an outsider in a world where church was a default setting. It was strange, being on the outside of that bubble. Especially as a person of faith. Because I hadn't lost God in all of this deconstructing. I just didn't feel great hanging out at His house anymore.

And then, one day as I was driving Ben home from soccer, he lobbed me another tough question.

"Momma, are we ever gonna go back to church?"

I had forgotten the moment that had sent me on this unraveling journey to begin with. How that initial snag in my sweater, which was now threadbare, began with a question from a car seat.

The decision to stay in church was harming my children. But my decision to leave? Well, I honestly hadn't considered that.

Ben's question was the first time I'd reconsidered.

The next was at Thanksgiving dinner.

My aunt somehow brought up the topic of Moses. Who knows why the heck that was involved in Thanksgiving, but it was, and my son asked a question. Isn't Moses the guy with the boat full of animals? In that moment, I could feel myself turning into Jell-O, and I wanted to melt down in my chair. I hadn't realized that this time away from church was, indeed, affecting my children. How, I wasn't entirely sure. But while I was the eager child with ten gold stars on my Bible verse memorization poster, my son didn't know who parted the Red Sea versus who drove an ark of creatures through it. My aunt looked at me and I looked back at her and then she looked back at me once more. I wasn't sure if it was concern or judgment in her eyes, but either way, I had something to consider. *Was my time as a homeless Christian harming my children? Was I being selfish?* All this time I was thinking I had shaken off shackles and become free of something that harmed me.

It's fine, I argued in my own brain. That story is twisted anyways. I'm fine with the fact that my son doesn't know about the genocide committed by God. And besides, half the posters that illustrate that story show dinosaurs hanging out with zebras. That didn't seem true, and if it wasn't entirely true, was it necessary to impart it to my child? What about the whole rainbow thing? I know how the Southern church spins that story. You can't escape the lesson of Noah without discussing the promise of a rainbow. And I never once heard that lesson preached without one throwaway insult at Pride.

You'll never change the meaning of GAWD'S RAINBOW!

I spent the rest of the Thanksgiving holiday in a parenting spiral of shame, googling church websites with my stomach in knots. I didn't exactly want to go back, but I also didn't want to fail my children.

That night, my pillow was perpetually hot. The covers never felt right. I was hot and cold, tossing and turning, in the kitchen for a fresh cup of water. The wheel in my brain spinning so fast it felt like the hamster had taken cocaine.

Sending my kids to church was to trust a complete stranger to teach them God's love. What if their teachers bastardized that lesson? It sure wouldn't be the first time. Far too often, I'd witnessed the Bible being used as a weapon against others. I'd seen it as a child with Purity Culture, and as an adult with my dear friend James. I'd seen it again with that "unity in the essentials" business that skirted hard questions. How could I possibly trust a church to spiritually guide my children?

After all (gestures everywhere) this?

By midnight my children were sound asleep, and I was still wrestling questions.

Had I thrown Baby Jesus out with the bathwater? Should I consider…finding fresh water? My experience with church had been 100 percent painful, but what if…there was a different kind of church? I felt bile rising up in my throat at the idea of sitting on a pew. It was the same feeling I had when Viggo Mortensen suggested I forgive my abuser. And that's exactly what the church had been to me. In a word, abusive. Knowing that, how could I ever risk returning—especially considering my children?

I sat in a cold sweat, processing this question and the hundreds that continued to follow. And then I ran right into the answer—like a Jeep tire meeting a squirrel.

What the hell, Joe?

After years of therapy and healing her wounds, my mom had moved on after my abuser. She fell in love with a man named Joe, and when we met him, we fell in love with him, too. For the last almost twenty years of my life, this man has redeemed the word *stepdad*. He is everything my childhood abuser was not—he's loving, kind, and safe. He's a grandfather to my children, and a father figure to me. He's a gentle and dear human being.

After all that pain, and betrayal, and harm…my mom finally found her safe place.

Maybe I could find a safe place, too. A church that was loving and gentle. A church that would show, not tell, the gospel. A church that would first do no harm. That welcomed questions and mess and people of every stripe. If God is love—and I believed that He was—then shouldn't His house be…loving?

A house of God that was worthy of the name.

What would that even look like?

When the pandemic started to putter out and the kids (finally) went back to school, there was a citywide competition sponsored by Google for elementary-age kids to design their "dream home."

Ben brought me a picture of his rendering one night, and he told me with great enthusiasm, "MOMMA! LOOK! I AM SO PROUD!"

So I read every detail, giggling at the milkshake machine and the pool full of fish. That's some Gatsby-level fancy. I was impressed.

And then, I noted the "wheelchair entrance." My heart couldn't handle the smile it contained. In my family, nobody uses a wheelchair. And to my knowledge, neither did any of Ben's classmates. It was such a small detail, but my eyes welled up with tears. It was such a loving detail.

"Ben, what made you think to include a wheelchair entrance in the design for your dream home?"

And without thinking or blinking, he shrugged and responded, "Well, if I'm making the perfect house, shouldn't everyone be able to come?"

Choking back tears, I took the picture from Ben and placed it on the fridge with a magnet.

"You know what, baby? I believe you are right. Everyone *should* be able to come."

· · · · · · · · · ·

Like any card-carrying Basic White Girl, my love for fall with its flannel and PSL everything runs deep. The irony being, I hate pumpkin spice. I just love how much other people love it. It's fun to celebrate the enjoyment of something (even if it tastes like burnt cinnamon).

Also, there's my annual trip in the fall with my best friends, Sara and Meredith. The changing leaves in New York and the excitement to see my friends never fail to turn me into Buddy the Elf the second I step off the plane. Buddy the Elf is not an exaggeration. Sara has grabbed me mid-twirl to remove me from the street on more occasions than I want to memorialize in print.

But summer. Summer has my heart. There's something about my kids and their friends running around, all of us free from the overscheduling of the school year. Throw in nights that were practically made for chips and salsa, and I'm hard-pressed to find a more perfect time of year.

The summer after our return to Alabama, my family joined a community pool. It's a beautiful place, on top of a mountain, where the kids run around all summer like characters in a Norman Rockwell painting. Somehow my kids got roped into joining the dive team, which to my delight was an hour-long practice twice a week, with meets on Saturdays. So, a bit of a commitment, but I didn't mind at all. In fact, diving is my favorite sport (from a strictly spectator perspective).

There's nothing like watching my six-year-old daughter waddle across the diving board, flick up her hands with that razzle-dazzle flourish, and then launch off the board with some sort of movement that is equal parts swan dive and belly flop. Give me a Coke Zero and a spot in the shade, and I can watch a youth dive team for hours.

And that's exactly what I was doing, minding my own business (as well as my hilarious kids), when the cutest two moms grabbed chairs next to me and started cheering for their little boy, Cal.

Now, as someone who is famously awkward in public, I'm not big on first impressions. But it was friends-at-first-sight with Jana and Jennifer. We started chatting and just...never stopped.

Jennifer and Jana are biscuits and gravy, well-paired but with obvious differences. The main difference being that one is a social butterfly, while the other prefers a cocoon. I adore this, because my bipolar behind relates to both, depending on the day of the week.

When I'm hypomanic and feeling social, I can count on Jennifer to sit by the pool and chatter with me like little June bugs about anything from life to faith to local politics to what we are planning for dinner. Then, when my energy inevitably changes, I can always recover with Jana. She's the best friend for sitting at an umbrella table in that "comfortable with quiet" kinda way.

It was an Eeyore at the umbrella table kinda day when Jana just popped the Question. It wasn't out of nowhere, but I still wasn't ready.

"Hey, would you like to go to church with me sometime?"

I swear, I blinked for a solid ten seconds before she decided to reframe the question.

"I mean, it's a pretty chill church and the pastor is great. You know John Mullaney, right? Anyways, I sing in the band on Sundays. You're welcome to join, whenever."

. . . .

Have you ever seen *Final Destination*?

A group of teens misses a flight with the rest of their class for their senior trip, and when the plane explodes, they all think they're lucky for cheating death. Before long, they find out that Death does not like being stood up. Just like that slug lady from *Monsters, Inc.*, he's watching—always watching.

One by one, Death taps each seemingly lucky teen on the shoulder. And then he launches a truck loaded with logs at their face. Death has a flair for theatrics.

God wasn't exactly trapping me in a tanning bed to teach me a lesson. Old Testament God might have, so thank You, Jesus. This was more like God reaching down to pop me upside the head and tell me I haven't outrun His love. Or His arm span. Chucking a pair of delightful lesbian pool pals at me was a wink to soften that pop.

I accepted the invitation to go to church. I didn't exactly skip through its doors. Part of me kind of expected a few logs through my windshield on the drive over. What got me through those doors, then? Just some good ol'-fashioned liberal guilt. This was not an invitation I could decline, because what the hell was I going to say?

"Sorry, Jana and Jennifer, I can't go to church with you. Church has been harmful to my gay friends."

The day arrived, and I walked into the church with apprehension. My guard was up, and I was ready for the worst. As I settled into my seat and looked around the room, I couldn't help but notice that the church was bustling with people from all walks of life. My anxious feelings began to dissipate, and I felt somewhat comforted by the diversity present in the room.

Jana led worship, and nobody blinked because of who she loved. They just sang along to her beautiful voice. My children and Cal ran around the pews with the energy of a thousand suns, but nobody frowned or wrote nasty emails to the pastor, and if they did, he never let us know.

I couldn't stop the tears or the relief that flowed when I got to the parking lot.

For the first time in a long time, I didn't feel like I had to run out the door or explain myself to anyone. But just as the relief was settling in, something else crept up behind it—this suffocating fear I'd been trying to keep at bay.

Go go gadget, anxiety attack.

It hit me before I even made it home. All those years of trauma, distrust, betrayal—they weren't just erased in one visit. My hands were shaking on the wheel, and my chest felt like it was closing in on itself.

This wasn't just about sitting in a pew, that's what I was coming to realize.

It was about opening myself up again, about exposing my children to a space that could potentially harm them as it had harmed me. Was I being reckless? Had I walked straight back into the lion's den?

It was my trauma talking, I knew that. But even as my body was feeling unsafe, my heart and my spirit were drawn in. What I experienced in that church was different—so different, in fact, that I found myself wanting more.

Now, if you like walking things back, be my guest.

Me? I personally hate it.

I pick a position, hunker down, and COMMIT with my heels in deep.

Things that I love? Everybody's gonna know.

Things that I hate? Same.

Call it passion; call it obstinance. It's probably a little bit of both. Whatever you call it, you won't be confused about where I stand on things, one way or the other. I'm not great about it, but I do try to stay in a posture of learning and evolving and considering. It's just that sometimes I get a little...passionate, ya know? Devoted. Okay, evangelical.

And when I do, I go all in. (I'm blaming my momma for this one.)

So this new experience of going to church and actually liking it was mighty inconvenient, given that I'd just become the poster girl for bagging on evangelicals. This was my entire personality now.

I'd accidentally created a brand.

But hold on, MK, I whispered to myself in my head, wheeling back. *One little visit to a church service with your pool pals does not a churchgoer make.*

This doesn't mean I'm one of those church people again, I reassured myself.

I was experimenting. Yeah. That was it. It was just the once…

But then I went back on another Sunday. And then another one. And I kept on liking it. Then I started getting to know people, and wouldn't you know it, I liked them, too.

Now this is becoming a problem.

I didn't know how to proceed. So I did what any self-respecting, church-grown Christian would do: I took my concerns to the principal's office.

I scheduled a meeting with the pastor.

John sat down across from me in his beat-up leather chair. He was serene, calm. I was immediately thrown off. Where was the bigger-than-life personality with the pithy church motto one-liner? You belong here! Welcome to the family! Transformation happens here!

"Mary Katherine, thanks for coming in. It's great to have time with you. What would you like to talk about?"

I took a deep breath. And then I started UNLOADING. I'd had six years of questions and fury and learning and gathering evidence. This was the moment. This was my *A Few Good Men* courtroom scene and I was going up against the evil colonel Nathan R. Jessep.

YOU CAN'T HANDLE THE TRUTH.

Except...John seemed to already know.

"Yeah, I get that," he said softly. "I understand why you'd get there."

Huh? My mind spun for a second. Buddy, this is the part where you're supposed to defend all the actions of the church and justify the evil that's been done in the name of religion because we're supposed to have church buildings and budgets and evangelism. I was ready for him to tell me how I'd gotten it wrong, or how I wasn't seeing the full picture.

But instead, John just...listened. There was no defensive stance, no Bible verse thrown at me like a dart. He didn't try to minimize my experiences or theologically explain them away. He just accepted them, like they were valid. It was jarring. I felt my defenses wobble a bit, unsure whether to lean in or bolt for the door.

This was new. It was strange. After all the church leaders I'd encountered who only ever wanted me to fall in line, here was someone who didn't see my questions as a threat.

I'd ask another doozy and John would just affirm, "Yeah, that's a tricky one. I struggle with that, too." And then he'd let that hang out there. No pat answer. No scriptural commentary script.

Clearly, we weren't getting anywhere.

I decided to take a different approach. "And here's another thing," I declared. "I'm tired of people I love being excluded by the church just because of who they love. I'm tired of all the membership requirements and signing off on all kinds of statements and the way that churches are so exclusionary and you have to be a card-carrying member to be part of the 'family.' It's ridiculous!"

John gave a soft nod and answered, "Agreed. That's why we have open Communion here. We're not in the business of vetting anyone who wants to be part of a community focusing on Jesus."

"Wait, what?" I exclaimed. "Is that a thing? Like, you don't make people sign up for some kind of member kind of thing to do all the churchy stuff?" My Southern Baptist roots stood on end.

John chuckled. "No, we don't gatekeep access to God. People are where they are in their lives. All are welcome at this table for as long as they want to come to this table. It's an open table."

I could feel the angry waters in my heart retreating, just ever so slightly. For years, the church had released upon me a storm of trauma and pain. And not that the rain would disappear overnight…but in this moment, I could feel something happening. A light breaking through all the storm clouds.

Because just like at my little boy's perfect dream home, at this church everyone was wanted. And while the message wasn't exactly painted across the sky in some grand-scale biblical gesture, it *was* printed on the church welcome sign.

All are welcome, in rainbow letters.

I felt pretty certain they meant it.

CHAPTER 10

Cheese Salad

One of my childhood Sunday school teachers called anything and everything her "ministry." She was the one who was leading that Jabez Bible study, praying for more responsibility.

She cared for children, so they were her ministry.

She deeply loved animals, so they were her ministry.

At one point, she got into rehabilitating old toys, and she even called that her ministry.

"Because if you love something enough, and it makes you love Jesus, that is a part of your ministry."

I hear you, Ms. Pat. But based on that definition, it's clear to me that after all this time...

Cheese is my ministry.

I love it with my whole heart, and whenever I eat it, I do a little dance in my chair. It makes me feel loved by God, as if He got to my soul through my stomach. But the vessel for that transport is always cheese.

A friend and I were discussing cheese the other day (this is what we talk about when we aren't blowing up the internet with diatribes about faith or mean people). She asked me to tell her what my favorite cheese is, and I was primed and ready to answer.

"Pimento!" I proclaimed.

She raised an eyebrow.

Suddenly, I was filled with misgivings. Because as I was saying it out loud, I realized that pimento's identity isn't super clear. It has cheese in it...but doesn't really get to live with the other cheeses on the shelf at the Piggly Wiggly. It usually hangs out with the dips and the spreads.

Wait a minute, I thought, doubt blooming in my heart. *Is pimento cheese not a real cheese?* When your ministry is cheese, but your favorite cheese isn't, you really have to pause and reflect.

And that's when I went down a rabbit hole, when I should have been doing any number of other things, like cleaning my house, writing this book, or drinking water for the first time in weeks. But deadlines be damned (and dirty floors, too) pimento shot straight to the top of my Google search history.

Turns out, most folks don't consider pimento cheese as a singular type of cheese. Because, wait for it, it's not. Sigh. I know, it hurts me to say that out loud. But, I feel like you need to know. Pimento cheese is a combo platter of shredded Cheddar, mayonnaise, and pimientos. (For the uninitiated, a pimiento is a kind of pepper. And it's delicious in cheese. You're welcome.)

And then I had a further revelation, and this is gonna rock your world.

Pimento cheese is a salad.

Now if you read that line and you understood, here's what I know about you: You're from the South.

If that line made no sense to you, bless your heart, and scoot up a chair.

In the South, especially in my part of Alabama, anything mixed with mayonnaise is a salad.

Say you've got diced chicken and mayonnaise. It's chicken salad.

Potatoes and mayo? Potato salad.

Tuna and mayo? Tuna salad.

Egg and mayo? Egg salad.

Unless you mash up the yolk of a boiled egg with mayo and then shove it back into its hollowed-out egg white. At which point it becomes a deviled egg. (Stuffed eggs if you're, say, Church of Christ.)

Sometimes the salad designation can get pretty controversial. Don't believe me? Try arguing with a Southerner about whether or not potato salad has raisins. For the record, it shouldn't—but in some corners of the South, it happens. (I know, I know, cue the banjos.)

I don't know which one of my Pilgrim cousins first found an old box of raisins and thought, *I could either throw these in the trash can where they belong, or I could throw them in some potato salad.* But they did, and they do, and now they are the laughing-stock of our mayo-colored ancestors.

And then there are the rest of the sane Southern folk, who agree that fruit is only for chicken salad (and even then, only sometimes).

Now, we aren't talking about spinach and strawberries with some feta and a breast of grilled chicken. Reminder that we're working with the Southern algebra of mayo + anything = salad.

I know, it can be confusing. Especially if you're a northerner.

So, let's say you're from Boston. And you're reading this thinking, *Uh, yeah. None of that is salad. Salad starts with a bowl of lettuce, not a bowl of mayonnaise.* And let's say you're right. (You aren't. I'm gonna stick to my definition. But let's say you are.)

If I buy your argument, that brings me to the perfect example of a cultural crossroads. Based on our collective defining of the word, coleslaw is salad salad. It's a bowl of lettuce + mayo, which then equals...you got it.

Salad salad.

I was standing in my local grocery store when I was given a revelation by God. Or maybe I was just a bit hyper-fixated on "essentials" after the New Hope disaster.

But have we ever defined, at its core, what is most essential in order to be called salad?

· · · · · · · · ·

Six years ago, I was invited by a big-time publisher to send in a book proposal. They'd seen a few of my silly, viral videos and heard that I was Christian. So, they'd decided to ask if I was interested in dipping my toe into book writing. What they didn't know was that not only was I interested, I had a pitch ready in my back pocket.

I'd been dying to write this specific book, and my proposal was already written. So when their email came in, I uploaded that document and smashed that send button like a bug.

Those folks were gonna drool over my book proposal. It was funny. It was fire. It was snarky.

The title: *Jesus Wasn't an Asshole.*

I awaited their enthusiastic response.

And waited a whole lot more.

Eventually, I did receive an email. It wasn't the one I was hoping for. Apparently, the Christian publishing industry is a biiiit like LifeWay Christian was (a lesson I hope they connect with in this book, because evolving is necessary for survival). Apparently, in this faith-based world some wordy durds are allowed—but they certainly can't be in the title.

That is a step too far.

It's a shame, honestly. It was a dang good idea, and the timing of the message was immaculate. Since that time, a few similar titles have been released, and the authors did amazing jobs. But in my humble, unbiased opinion, none had the spark of my initial proposal.

I mean, c'mon. You know you would buy that title (if not just to mail to your uncle).

When the editor reached out to relay this rejection, he proposed an alternate title. And when I responded that the word *meanie* wasn't gonna cut it, he delivered my final letdown.

The book just wasn't a good fit, anyways. It wasn't personal; he wished me well. And maybe, if I kept writing and trying, I could swing it as a "secular" writer.

Yes, that man legit called me "secular," and no, I didn't take it with grace. Let's just say that your girl was triggered. 'Cause to this bona fide (former) Baptist youth group leader, "secular" is a helluva insult.

So, I dropped some biblical knowledge in response, which I was certain would change his mind. It didn't, and I'm lucky the whole interaction didn't end my career instead.

Anyways, that letter went something like this (and sir, if you're reading...I'm not sorry).

Dear Eddy McEditor,

I understand that secular crass talk is frowned upon—but what about biblical crass talk? Is that allowed? Because, man, do I have some zingers for you. I submit for your consideration, (with a little bit of paraphrasing):

Pinky Dink? (1 Kings 12:10) "My little finger is thicker than my father's loins."

Son of a Hoebag Rebel? (1 Samuel 20:30) "Saul's anger flared up at Jonathan and he said to him, 'You son of a perverse and rebellious woman!'"

Stanky Lips (Job 19:17–19) "My breath is strange to my wife, and I am a stench to the children of my own mother."

Donkey Dong (Ezekiel 23:20) "There she lusted after her lovers, whose genitals were like those of donkeys and whose emission was like that of horses."

Please advise if these updated language samples will work for your publishing house.

Blessings,

Mary Katherine Backstrom

So a few things. I will acknowledge right off the bat that don-key dong isn't exactly an "insult." But I felt that its crassness supported my point. And that horse emissions bit?

Ew, David.

It seemed to me the term "a-double-s-hole" couldn't step in the ring with Old Testament insults. Not even in the same freaking weight class. But I guess my old rule book on Christian Pearl Clutchery was missing a couple of chapters.

Meh.

So, that book proposal died a slow, sad death of being starved for attention in my outbox. And then I wrote *Holy Hot Mess*. An uplifting, sunny, storytelling book. Nary a bad word in sight. That editor must've known a little something about market, because that book was a national bestseller.

Which means, after tucking my humor and my words in tight, and learning to edit my voice...I was finally allowed to don the proud label of Best-selling Christian Author.

And I mean it when I tell you that I'm proud of that label.

But I kinda don't know what it means?

Best-selling, I get. I worked my tail off for that. And author, that's obvious. You're reading my book.

But Christian? How was that designation handed out?

Who was in charge of passing out holographic fish stickers in the publishing world? What was their decision-making matrix, ya know?

I mean, you can't go slapping CHRIST FOLLOWER on just anyone.

What if they don't believe in hell?

What if they do, and they say I am going?

What if they thought speaking a few cusswords was "using the Lord's name in vain," but bastardizing the Lord's name for political purposes was "winning our country for Jesus"?

Seriously, asking for a friend.

Whoever was gatekeeping the "Christian" label had a system I couldn't discern. Best I could tell, their line was drawn somewhere between "shit" and "jiminy cricket."

That ambiguity gnawed at me more than I wanted to admit. I knew the label "Christian" meant something important to me once, but now? I wasn't sure what it stood for anymore. And that made me question whether I even fit into the box that people had neatly labeled me with. Was I still Christian by their standards, or mine?

I decided to get some answers.

Remember that church I had started going to? The one with the kindhearted pastor? I decided I trusted him just well enough to attempt an unannounced drop-in. I busted up in John Mullaney's office with a mouthful of coffee and questions. I may or may not have just started on Vyvanse, so throw a little stimulant in, too. My insides were itchy and my outsides were agitated. I needed to get some answers.

"Hey, John!" I walked in like I owned the place and sat in his twisty brown chair.

"Hey, MK! So glad to see you. What's up? Is everything good?"

"Yes, but I have a question to ask you—and I don't want you to be offended."

"Go on."

"You know that I left my previous churches because they were abusive and harmful."

"Yes."

"And you know that my deconstruction journey started when Ben asked me a question that I couldn't answer."

"Yes, about hell; I remember."

"And you know that as a parent, I love my children more than life itself."

"Yes."

"And you think that the current power structure of church in America does harm to all sorts of people?"

"Yes."

I was starting to feel a bit nervous. The next question was a bit out of pocket.

"Okay, I'm not asking you this as a pastor…I'm asking you this as a dad."

I paused, and John leaned back in his chair, ready for whatever was next.

"Knowing all the trauma that church can impart…why do you bring your kids here?"

John sighed and sat back in his chair. He shared his belief that the prominence of abuse is connected to exclusive power structures. That anytime an entire group of people are excluded from positions of authority, it creates a dynamic where few or no advocates exist to protect that community.

"I taught my daughters to look for red flags. You know, like that guy on TikTok?" John waved his imaginary flag. "No women in positions of authority? Red flag. No diversity in the congregation? Red flag. Disallowing a vote because of any identity? Red flag, red flag, red flag."

I found myself enjoying this game. I decided to join in the fun.

"Handling snakes?"

"Red flag," John laughed.

"Purity Culture?"

"Red flag."

"Complementarianism?"

"Red flag for me."

"Dancing with banners?"

"Green flag, are you kidding?"

I imagined sweet John, in his Methodist robes, dancing onstage with a ginormous banner. The picture made my heart very happy.

So, banner dancing is officially on my list. Nonessential, but definitely an upsell.

Betrayal. Judgment. Condemnation. Vague statements about "unity in essentials."

Add these things in big bold letters to the list of things I'm not looking for.

But over the last few years, I'd longed for a family. I wanted to be with believers. Once or twice I came out of my hermit hole, blinking. After all the abuse, disappointment, and hurt...I was starting to wonder: *What's out there?*

And then I was dragged from my isolation by the likes of Jana and Jennifer. I felt like a groundhog ripped out of the dark. It was all so much to take in. And yet, there was comfort in the warmth of community. It was starting to feel like sunshine.

Then a thought popped up that scared me to pieces:

Maybe I should try again.

But I needed something drastically different from before, and how was I going to do that? I knew exactly what I wasn't looking for, and not a dang clue of what I needed. How could I find a safe church home if I wasn't even able to describe it?

I tried to imagine a scenario in which this would work on any level.

"Sir, I was robbed; he just got away! I need a sketch artist, quick!"

"Sure thing; what did the bad guy look like?"

"Well, he wasn't tall and he wasn't blond and he didn't have an accent either."

That'd narrow it down, but not by a lot.

Good luck finding that guy.

If I was going to find a happy church home, there was no other way around it: I needed to finally establish essentials. Not some hokeypokey kumbaya version. But some hard standards, requirements, expectations.

And that's where I was stuck. After all these years of deconstructing, I knew everything I was running from. But what was I running toward? The answer to that question was falling into place.

I was looking to understand my values. The nonnegotiable, baseline requirements that a church must hold fast if I was going to feel safe.

And I don't mean the "Christian values" that are chucked up by greedy politicians who don't know the meaning of the phrase. I needed a church who knew their essentials—and lived them out with kindness. A place that nurtured souls, instead of sending them out needing therapy.

An answer was starting to float to the surface, and it was so unexpectedly simple. Clearly, I was looking for a church where love was unconditional. Never weaponized. Where love was the beginning and the end of every message, every action, every Sunday morning greeting.

I wasn't sure if my little Methodist church was the One, or just a kindhearted, gentle rebound.

What I knew was that when I was there, I always, always felt loved.

Maybe that was my first essential: love.

It felt like a good place to start.

CHAPTER 11

The Truth About Zebras

Dothan, Alabama, is the kind of small town that isn't aware that it's small. I know this is true, because anytime I refer to my hometown as "a small town in south Alabama," some native from the area is quick to respond, "Well, actually, we just got a Target."

But here's the thing about growing up in a We-Just-Got-a-Target-sized town: There isn't much to get into—besides church or trouble—so that is what everyone does. They party or they pray, or they try to do both, which results in enjoying neither. Dothan is a town that really wants a good time but feels too guilty to have it.

And in that way, Dothan and I were practically made for each other. At least in my formative teenage years, when I spent most of my time at church. Something I've noticed about small-town kids is they're all just a little bit unhinged. The slow pace of life and that teenage angst come together like opposing weather fronts, and every weekend the air is thick with an energy that has to get out.

The party crowd had it easy enough, chugging beers in peanut fields. They'd sneak Bud Light out of their parents' garage, drive to a classmate's farm, and a few cans later they had just enough courage to kiss a stranger, or perhaps pick a fight. The fire and the booze offered just enough adventure to quiet their hungry souls. At least until the following Saturday, when the electricity gathered once more.

But I was a church kid, so I couldn't party. Jesus had saved me from drinking Bud Light, but He hadn't laid out any other good options, which meant when I needed to let off some steam…I got into all sorts of shenanigans. Standard trouble was always available to the cooler, beer-drinking kids. But when church kids wanted to feel alive, we had to go make weird trouble.

If you ever made friends with a pastor's kid, you know exactly what I mean by Weird Trouble. It's hard to believe that any of us survived those youth group years. We did so much stupid, reckless shit: cow tipping, street sledding, sneaking onto trains… things that could 100 percent get us killed, but not put a stain on our souls.

Looking back, I imagine that Jesus would have probably preferred we drink the damn beer. But with frontal lobes that weren't fully developed, and the looming threat of damnation, my friends and I continued to chase Weird Trouble, which was dangerous but technically not sinful.

And this strategy was working just fine for everyone, until I went off and killed a dang zebra.

One of the most interesting hangouts in town was a place called Spanish Acres—it was a gas station that doubled as a tourist destination, which is very much a thing in the South. Now to be clear, I'm not talking about one of those huge truck stops that have a Pizza Hut, showers, and card games. Those places are great, and they have everything you need, but that's exactly what makes them forgettable.

Spanish Acres had a zebra. An actual zebra. It lived in the yard directly behind the gas station, with a big purple billboard announcing its presence.

COME TO SPANISH ACRES! SEE OUR ZEBRA!

With an arrow pointing down at the fence. And there he would stand, munching on grass, directly beneath his own billboard. That was the whole schtick, and it worked like a charm. I suppose it's basic psychology. Nobody decides "I need to get gas" and then feels particularly excited at the thought. But "I need to get gas, and I can go pet a zebra"?

Take our money, Spanish Acres.

Take. Our. Money.

I was three left turns from the school parking lot. That detail will forever stick out in my mind. Not in an "Oh, I was almost to school—why did this happen" kind of way. But in an "Ever since my first crash, my horn has been broken, and now every time I take a left turn, the horn won't stop honking" kind of way.

It was a rainy day, and I was already late, trying to make up for lost time. I'd left home at seven, which gave me thirty minutes to get across town to my high school, which would have been plenty of time if not for the rain, and the way high school students drove in it. Then, I got stuck behind a peanut tractor, and that was the final blow. I sighed as traffic backed up farther and farther, cars wrapping around the whole school. Three left turns, two traffic lights, one of which never turned green. I was gonna be tardy, no matter what.

Maybe I could come up with an excuse.

One of the benefits of being a natural-born storyteller is that when you're in trouble, you have this magical ability to cover your ass with a lie. I'm not proud of it; I'm just saying it's a thing. I could probably get out of this tardy.

But one of the downsides of being a good storyteller is that God gives you allll the weird stuff. I like to believe that He does it out of love. Like, "Oh that kid of Mine sure loves to tell stories—so I'm gonna give her a good one!"

I don't remember the moments that led to the crash, but I imagine it went something like this: I was deep in my brain trying to spin a good story that my physics teacher would believe, when my eyeballs saw danger and tried to tell my brain, but my brain was too busy lying. So the very important message of SLAM ON YOUR BRAKES didn't get through with nearly enough time.

I do remember the moment my tires started screaming, and my car skidded straight toward the trailer.

SMACK.

In the moments that immediately followed the wreck, the world seemed to go in slow motion. I wasn't hurt, and I hadn't died, but I could feel myself floating upward. Just far enough away to watch everything happen, and just close enough to physically do it. I'd later learn that this was disassociation, a natural response to any trauma—but at the time, all I knew was that something felt off, and information kept coming at me in batches.

Batch #1: My airbag didn't deploy. *That's good*, I think. *Ouch, my head hurts. Maybe it's not good.*

Batch #2: My horn is still honking. *Oh my God, everyone is out of their cars.*

Batch #3: They're staring at me. *No, not me. They're staring at the zebra in the trailer.*

Batch #4: Ohmygod ohmygod. *OHMYGOD, THERE'S A ZEBRA IN THAT TRAILER.*

It was that specific detail—a stripey little butt—that snapped my brain back to reality. That and the symphony of blue lights and sirens that were now pulling in on all sides.

The school bell was ringing, now. Eight in the morning.

I was definitely going to be tardy.

But Mr. Hughes, I killed a zebra and was surrounded by cops!

…That one might actually work.

I burst into physics class twenty minutes late, with tears streaming down my face. Tears that were more frenetic than sad, because honestly? I was still processing. When I finally left the scene of the crime, the zebra was still in its trailer. The owner kept peeking in, and I heard mention of a vet, but I felt the situation was dire. I mean, the entire police force doesn't usually show up for a teenager in a bumper bender. (I would know. I had more than a few.)

But this time was different. I'd killed a zebra. And not just any zebra...a famous one. Technically, I couldn't be sure he was dead. It's not like they rolled him away on a stretcher, with a leg hanging out from under the blanket.

But my anxiety was 100 percent certain. And since I listen to my anxiety over any other voice in my head, this was the tale I believed:

I was a killer. An accidental killer, sure, but I doubted that detail would do much to assuage the heartbreak at Spanish Acres. Whatever legacy I'd made in this town, it was forever and irreversibly tarnished. There was no coming back from this. I wanted to throw my keys into the sun, or perhaps I should just throw myself. Instead, I threw myself into a desk and prepared for my moment of shame.

Mr. Hughes paused a beat before setting down his chalk. He sighed, causing his mustache to twitch, then adjusted his round rimmed glasses. He looked like a disappointed owl, and I understood his disappointment.

"Mary Katherine, is everything...okay? I'm gonna need a note from the office."

"Oh my God, the note! I'm sorry, Mr. Hughes; I forgot to stop at the office!"

In a moment of panic, I shot up from my seat, unleashing the next phase of chaos. The desk, which was somewhat attached to my body, followed me across the floor, screeching loudly as it dragged against the tile until, finally, both of us fell. Books and body parts and Diet Mountain Dew all landed on the floor with a thunk. And that was the straw that broke my camel. Not the thunk, but the gasps of my classmates.

Butt up, desk down, and surrounded on all sides by my personal belongings, I wanted to melt into the floor. I lay there a minute, in a pile of my own shame, just wishing for the Rapture to come. But there was no trumpet, no planes crashing down, no Jesus coming to save me. At least not from this particular crisis. I groaned and stood up from the floor, peeling the desk off my legs.

"I…I just…"

The water was rumbling behind the dam. One more word and the levees would break. I took a deep breath, trying to regain control of myself and the whole situation.

Mr. Hughes was frozen, with his head slightly tilted, out of confusion or concern or who knows what. But it was that detail, that little head tilt, that shoved me over the edge. I'd just killed a zebra, and my teacher looked like an owl, and my stuff was all over the floor.

It was funny enough that I wanted to laugh, and horrible enough that I wanted to cry. It was too many feelings, all at once, for my brain to process correctly. You know, like when you have eight thousand strings of Christmas tree lights plugged into the same little socket, and you think it's gonna work fine…but then there's a pop, and a puff of black smoke, and the power in the house goes out? Then you flip the switch and the grid reboots and everything in the kitchen goes beep at the same time?

That, I think, is what happened to my brain. There were too many plugs in the outlet.

"I killed the zebra," I announced to the world. It was all I could think to say. Then POP went the weasel; my grid was rebooting with ALL of the beeps in the kitchen.

I was sobbing, laughing, hiccupping, coughing, choking on my own dang spit. The owl looked like he might hack up a mouse.

"That's what the cop cars were all about?"

I nodded my head in response.

"You killed the zebra...from Spanish Acres?"

I nodded my head at that, too.

The room was quiet, so freaking quiet, I could practically hear their eyeballs. And what I couldn't hear, I could definitely feel. They were boring into my skin.

Was I a zebra murderer?

I could neither confirm nor deny it. I had to imagine that animals in trailers wouldn't fare well in an accident. But I also hadn't seen some sad ambulance veterinarian lift a hoof for a pulse before solemnly declaring a time of death. If prestige cable dramas of the last fifteen years have taught us anything it's this: If we haven't seen the body, then we haven't seen the crime, and we know nothing, Jon Snow.

There is a truth in every lie we tell. Even the lies we tell ourselves. Ask any (honest) nonfiction writer if their books are 100 percent true. They'll say yes, then start throwing out all sorts of caveats.

It's not not true.

It's my truth.

It's truth...but not the whole story.

It reminds me of how every year when I was growing up, Third Baptist Church did a production of the Christmas story called *Living Portraits*. It was the mannequin challenge, set in a manger, as imagined by first world Baptists.

My senior year, a cute guy at church was holding a sign-up sheet, pleading for students to help with the program, on behalf of his choir director mom. Maybe I felt bad for him, or maybe it was a crush. All I know is I signed the dang sheet, figuring at most I'd be playing a donkey, or offstage dangling a star from a fishing pole.

Y'all, they cast me to be the Virgin Mary.

I sure hadn't seen that coming.

It's embarrassing to admit, but for a youth groupy church kid this was somewhat of a status symbol. Last year's Mary was Miss Alabama, and the Mary before that became prom queen. One doesn't simply get cast in this role. One is chosen to carry the mantle. The news hit the pews the following Sunday when the cast was announced in the bulletin. After church, a whole flock of the big-money blue-hairs came over to hug and congratulate me, as if I had gotten engaged.

"Are you nervous?"

"It's such an important role!"

"My granddaughter played Mary when she was your age, and now she's a dermatologist!"

I was starting to regret that five-minute crush I had on the sign-up-sheet boy. It was all a bit much, this popularity pipeline, full of pageant queens and dermatologists. I'd drastically over-shot my donkey ambition, and I wasn't sure how I felt about it.

The day of the show, the cast arrived at the church a few hours early. The choir director marked our places and offered simple instructions:

"Get to the stage before your song, and don't move 'til the music is over!"

One scene, one song. Easy enough.

"Virgin Mary you're up next! Are you ready? Here's your baby!"

"I'm ready!" I replied, grabbing the bundle. I glanced at my notes one more time:

The Virgin Mary stands at center stage, holding Baby Jesus. She looks upon the face of Jesus, is immediately overwhelmed.

The orchestra swelled and my song was beginning. I walked to my mark on the stage.

"Mary, did you know..."

I looked down at my precious baby, and per the director's notes, I was immediately overwhelmed.

Hand to God, my little baby Jesus was an actual Cabbage Patch Kid. Red hair, freckles, wrapped in swaddling clothes.

Holy. Baby. Chucky.

It was nearly impossible to choke back laughter, so I did what any reasonable person would do in that situation: I tried to make myself sad. I imagined my dog was running away, and that helped. At least I wasn't laughing.

But then my brain was like *This is a fun game; let me help! How sad would it be if your dog DIED?*

And my emotions were like *DID SOMEBODY SAY DOGS DIE?*—and anyways, halfway through the song I was crying onstage like an idiot. The snot and tears were perfectly synced with the swell of the final verse. It worked. The congregation was utterly moved.

"WOW! That performance was exquisite! You perfectly captured the emotions of a new mother! What were you thinking about?"

"It was a lot," I said. Which was a terrible answer, so I sprinkled a little cheese on top. "I tried to imagine how Mary would feel, holding Baby Jesus."

Boy, was the church impressed with me, my tears, and my heart for the Lord.

They'd never know the whole truth with its creepy freckled face. About Chucky Doll Jesus or my hypothetically dead dog. Or at least, that's what I was hoping at the time—I was becoming quite proud of my newly minted status as the Youth Group Icon.

It's funny, isn't it, how we can embellish a story—or leave out the odd detail here or there—and suddenly it takes on a new, exciting life. It's a skill that my brain has utilized well, hence the reason I'm a bang-up storyteller. But those details can come back and haunt you like ghosts, especially when folks start asking questions.

I remember when *Holy Hot Mess* was released and I started having daily panic attacks, because I had read a story about this guy who wound up in Oprah's Book Club, but then everyone found out that he lied in his book, and the townspeople gathered with pitchforks.

And this was new to me, all this author business. Nobody gave me a rule book. I told my story as best I knew how, and in a few places I fudged the details. I mean, small details, hot dogs instead of hamburgers kinda stuff. Nothing that ruined the integrity of the story. From my perspective. If anyone's asking.

But for real, what's allowed in an autobiography? Any flourish? Or is it facts, only?

Because if you're mining from nothing but perfectly preserved memories...well, good luck with that source material. Half of my life was affected by trauma. My memories look a lot like Swiss cheese, and that's when I'm seeing them clearly.

What about the places that I had to fill in? The places my brain rewired things? If I didn't get it right—down to the detail, would I be accountable?

And if so...to whom?

I imagined myself standing up onstage, hugging my new friend, Oprah. *Holy Hot Mess* being featured in the book club, when suddenly some form of fact-checking SWAT team rappels down from the studio rafters.

"WHERE IS MARY KATHERINE BACKSTROM?"

"ARE YOU MARY KATHERINE BACKSTROM?"

"WHAT WAS IT, LADY?"

"WAS IT A HOT DOG OR A HAMBURGER?"

"DID THE ZEBRA DIE OR DIDN'T HE?"

And I'd get all squirmy, because all of a sudden "It was my truth" isn't the philosophical mic drop I thought it would be when presented with this situation.

Time went by and out from under the horrified gaze of my peers, the zebra story sort of became my thing. I busted it out at parties and picnics and PTA meetings—anywhere I hoped to charm potential friends and figured I could retell this in a quirky "Oh, MK," way.

Decades later, I found myself back in Dothan on my first ever book tour. Returning to my hometown with my dream job and my very own book jacket. It felt like I'd stepped into a Meg Ryan movie and I leaned hard into the nostalgia of it all. A Diet Coke in my cupholder, I drove around to hit a few landmarks in my own *This Is Your Life*.

It was all still there. The peanuts, the people, the tractors. The churches. My favorite Mexican restaurant, La Bamba.

But three lights from my high school, something was missing.

Where was Spanish Acres?

Had I cost the poor souls who owned the gas station their zebra and their livelihood?

Distraught over the consequences of my carnage, I posted online to find out what exactly had happened to Spanish Acres, even though I wasn't sure what I would do with that information. Make amends, maybe?

To my absolute shock, the owner of the gas station found my post and commented.

Now, before what I'm about to tell you gets taken the wrong way, please keep in mind: I know this is good news, and at my core, I am happy about it.

But that freaking zebra lived.

It lived a long time. Like twenty-something more years. If you don't know much about zebras (like I clearly do and not because I just googled it), they live to be about twenty-five years old. Which means that zebra not only lived, but it lived a whole daggum zebra life.

The gas station? Sold to developers. The owner then had money, *and* she didn't have to clean up zebra poop or card teenagers for nicotine anymore.

Everyone involved lived happily ever after.

Except me.

Because now my fantastical zebra story was happy and boring and completely wrecked.

What was I supposed to do with that?

The truth is, I grew up in a family of storytellers. Listening to stories around our Thanksgiving table is like watching the movie *Big Fish*—it's hard to separate fact from fiction.

For example, like every other white girl below the Mason-Dixon Line, I grew up hearing that I was the great-great-granddaughter of some beautiful Cherokee princess. Later I was told, No...we actually came from an Irish pirate. Then, in the Christmas family newsletter that my grandmother typed up and mailed to everyone back in 1998, these two stories were combined and this questionable heritage became canon.

I remember having my doubts about all of it, especially the Native American bit. I have the skin tone of an uncooked biscuit and I cook like a lobster in the shade. But whenever I expressed my doubts I was shhh'ed in response and told, "That's just the Irish in you."

Last Christmas, my cousins took a DNA test that just about got us on *Maury*. Turns out, our family has been lying all this time, which my uncle dismissed as fake news. We are 100 percent saltine crackers. Not even the fancy kind. We are descendants, not of pirates or princesses, but of run-of-the-mill, sunburned Pilgrims.

The truth turned out to be a little disappointing. Not that I hadn't suspected it. But sometimes, I guess the delusions we create are more exciting than our reality.

So, we tell ourselves fantastical stories to avoid facing all the hard stuff. Or at least, that's what my family does. I suspect we aren't alone in this. Okay, maybe the bits about zebras and princesses—but the rest of it? Let's all be honest.

In the stories of our lives—at least the ones we tell ourselves—there's always some fact and some fiction.

It's not knowing the difference, believing our own bullshit…

That can reaaaaally get us into trouble.

CHAPTER 12

Not That Wheel, Jesus!

I was supposed to be sitting beneath an umbrella, watching my kids at the beach. Or sitting with Ian, celebrating our seventeenth wedding anniversary over a nice steak dinner. Or maybe just reading a book on the porch as the storms rolled in from the ocean. I should've been doing a lot of things on this precious little family vacation.

But not this.

Not crying in a shady gas station parking lot in the middle of Nowhere, Florida, with my kids strapped into their car seats. I told Ben and Holland we were stopping for gas, and to please just stay in the car. They didn't ask questions, but I could tell they wanted to.

Very clearly, something was wrong.

If I'm being honest, things had been off between Ian and me for a good long while. We had grown distant, not in any explosive way, but in the kind of slow drift that happens when you stop paying attention. It was the little things—like the way we'd eat dinner in separate rooms or go to bed without touching or talking, like roommates. I had been wrestling with questions in therapy, exploring the foundations of my faith, while his mind was in an entirely different orbit. We'd come home from our separate days just to sit separately on the couch with the TV filling in the silence between us. We fought about money, but what couple doesn't? I hadn't wanted to see it. I didn't want to confront the possibility that the life we had built, the one I was so deeply proud of, was crumbling beneath the surface. So I ignored the distance, and I rewrote the narrative.

Same zebra, different stripes.

I told myself we were busy, that this was just life with kids. Marriages go through phases, and this one was challenging but it wasn't anything we couldn't work through.

That morning, Ian and I had spent several hours on the beach, playing in the ocean with the kids. The memories in my camera roll from that morning are picture-perfect, but the truth is I knew the entire day that something was seriously sideways. We had come on this vacation hoping to reconnect, to wash away the tension that had been building. It was supposed to be a reset. Ian had always loved the sea, and although I'm not much for dark moving water where creatures with sharp teeth are swimming, I joined him in the ocean for a couple of hours in a bid to close the emotional gap between us. But even as we bobbed in the water side by side, I could feel the whole ocean was between us. When we packed up our things and made our way to the parking lot, he was walking almost ten yards ahead of me.

Still, I thought it was no big deal. We were in a funk. And funks can be fixed, right? We'd gone through rough patches before, so why should this be any different?

When we got back to his parents' house, the kids had dinner and settled into watching a movie, so I asked my husband if we should go for a walk around the block, thinking that maybe some alone time could thaw the ice between us.

I reached for his hand, but it felt stiff and forced. I was holding the hand of a stranger. Looking back, I should have known that was the moment. We made a little small talk, which quickly devolved into an argument about I don't know what…and then, we hadn't walked past five mailboxes when he blurted out "I want a divorce."

We'd both used the *d* word over the years once or twice, mostly in the heat of an argument. But never had it resulted in any sort of action…it was more of an angry suggestion. But this time, it didn't sound like a suggestion. In his voice, the word sounded like a promise. And I knew, in that moment, that what I felt didn't matter. Our marriage was over for him.

My head was spinning as I turned back. I couldn't process what had just happened. I walked back to the house and hugged his parents. I packed the kids up and loaded the car. Tears streamed down my face as I pulled out of the driveway. We'd left without saying goodbye.

And now, here I was, crying at a gas station, staring down at my phone with shaky hands. I called my mom, praying she would answer.

"Hello?" Her voice was the final straw. The levees inside me were buckling.

"Mom, the kids and I are coming back home. No, listen. The vacation is over. I need you and Joe to get on the road and meet us halfway, in Atlanta."

"Baby, what in the world is happening?"

I struggled to choke back the sobs.

"It's over, Momma. He wants a divorce."

There was a pause on the other end of the line, the kind that only happens when someone is trying to find the right words for a heartbreak they can't fix. I could hear the sound of her grabbing the keys, the familiar jingle somehow grounding me to the moment.

"Okay, baby. I'm on the way. Joe and I will meet you halfway. Just hold on, all right? We'll be there."

"Thank you, Momma."

I nodded even though she couldn't see me, then ended the call and took a deep breath. Two hundred more miles to carry this secret in a car with two confused kids. Surely, I could hold it together for them, at least for the next couple of hours.

I wiped my face and got back in the car, pausing to collect my thoughts, then looked at my kids with a smile.

"Who wants to play some Disney trivia?"

"Meeeee!" they responded in unison.

I shoved that grief down deep in my body, and, pulling back

onto the interstate, I did my best to come up with small questions about *Aladdin*, *The Lion King*, and Epcot.

I don't remember much about the drive except the monotony of the highway, but eventually, we arrived at a hotel in Atlanta, where Momma and Joe were waiting. They helped me settle the kids into bed, and after a hot shower, I found myself lying down, staring at the ceiling. The room was quiet, but inside my head, there was a storm brewing.

I was racking my brain for answers to questions I'd been avoiding asking out loud. In therapy, I had started to explore the possibility that my marriage was seriously broken. My therapist had been gently guiding me to that question, and I suppose she knew the truth long before I did.

"You're going to have to pull back the delusions," she had said. "Once you do, *everything* will probably start to unravel. But that's how the healing begins."

As my mom drove me closer and closer to town, anxiety was pressing in. By the time I stepped through our blue front door, my stomach was churning with dread.

Everything happy in our home was now just a shattered delusion. How could it all be over?

In our closet were his clothes, which would soon be in boxes. His protein shakes were in the fridge. Portraits hung on the wall of a smiling family unit that no longer existed.

I ripped down the pictures and put them in the garage. In a way, it helped me feel seen. I was a zombie, and our home was my sepulchre. Let these barren walls share in my misery.

But still, once a day, I would sneak back into the garage (as if someone was watching me do it). And I'd cry and cry over the piles of frames.

I was stuck in my grief. Lost in confusion.

We were a happy family...right?

Each frame held a snapshot of the life I thought I had, the life I had carefully crafted in my mind. But now, I was starting to see the reality behind the beautiful smiles. Behind the staged, perfect pictures of happiness. The truth was always hiding in plain sight. There had always been turmoil beneath the surface. Years of miscommunication, immaturity, and struggle. Of disconnect, hurt, and resentment.

As I took down the pictures, I felt like I was deconstructing the careful delusion of the perfect marriage I had built. The castle was falling apart piece by piece, and so was the narrative I'd spun in my head and even online for my audience. It was so fantastic, so beautiful, so thoughtfully crafted...and so far removed from the reality of things.

For the next several days, I existed in a fog. I felt nausea in the center of my chest. I'd never felt so deeply lonely, so utterly hollow.

Where was God in my darkest of valleys?

I wasn't even sure where to turn in my faith anymore, and I was tired of asking hard questions. Sure, I had wanted to get to the truth of things, but this truth felt too unkind to face. I was left with the truth, laid bare like I wanted. One tug, and he'd unraveled everything.

It was time to face the fact that my life would never be healthy or happy unless I started to see things for what they really were—in every aspect of my life.

If I wanted to rebuild to find clarity and truth, I had to start by tearing down the lies I was telling myself, to let go of the delusions I still clung to.

And this, my marriage, was the most painful one.

Not that wheel, Jesus. Not that one.

CHAPTER 13

Chasing Snakes

I was never an outdoorsy person before my divorce.

My friends called me an "indoor cat."

And it's true: I preferred a domesticated environment—air-conditioning, fluffy pillows, a fridge full of leftovers and snacks. But when my marriage fell apart, I did something that was part Bella Swan, part Forrest Gump. One day, I found myself hiking on a trail in the woods, and then, you know what? I just kept hiking.

I spent hours each day out there, in the thick of the trees, searching for God knows what. At first, it was a mile, then seven, then thirteen. At one point, I was hiking fifteen miles a day, surviving off Gatorade and tuna kits. I hiked until there were holes in my shoes—and in the next pair of shoes after that. Even a stress fracture in my foot couldn't stop me. The doctor put me in a boot, but two days later, I left it at home and headed back to my "happy place." Stress fracture be damned; I was a woman on a mission. But even to me, that mission was unclear.

Sure, the weight loss got me compliments. People started telling me how amazing I looked, how they admired my "bounce-back" from the divorce. My shrinking waistline seemed to make them believe I was healing—maybe even thriving. In their eyes, my physical transformation was a signal that I was shedding all my grief along with the pounds.

But deep down, I knew that wasn't the case. If I was honest with myself, I was still running—from my emotions, from accountability, from the hard truths I wasn't ready to face. Somewhere in the back of my mind, I was still waiting. Hoping, maybe, that he'd find me out there one day—walk up beneath the canopy of trees and say, "I love you. Let's work this out." I imagined it so many times: yellow leaves raining down around us, the kiss that would seal it all back together. I'm not saying I played it all out in my head...I'm just saying, *That's how it would go.*

As I walked, I would ruminate on what I could have done differently to make it all work. I wondered, What was his perspective of why things were broken? If I understood that, I could change all my pieces to fit better into the relationship.

So I kept walking. Fall turned to winter, winter to early spring, and still, he never found me out there. But by then, the trails had become my obsession—my escape from the outside world.

The miles added up. My body grew lean, but my spirit was thinning, too, stretched by the weight of all the unanswered questions. In the midst of my compulsive hikes, my therapist asked to see me for a "special appointment." She wasn't celebrating my weight loss, not even close. She looked at me with concern. Words like *ruminate*, *obsessive*, and *unhealthy* drifted into the air between us, and her expression was one of deep worry—which is always extra alarming when it's coming from a therapist.

"Have you ever been bitten by a snake?" she asked out of nowhere.

I didn't think so, but I figured if I had, that was something I'd probably remember. "No," I said, a little smirk on my face, because I always loved her weird questions.

"Imagine you've been bitten by a snake. A venomous one—a rattler." She paused. "Your foot hurts, the snake's venom is spreading, and it's slithered off that way." She gestured vaguely. "What are you going to do?"

This was easy. I pictured the wound, the swelling, and the thick brown timber rattler disappearing into the brush. "Call 911," I said immediately.

She tilted her head slightly. "Really? You wouldn't go chase down the snake?"

The question caught me off guard, but I laughed. "Of course not. Why would I do something stupid like that?"

She shrugged. "Maybe to pick it up? To ask it questions like, 'Why did you bite me?' or to convince it to apologize. Would that make you feel better?"

The laughter stopped. I knew where this was going. "Just to be clear, in this story, my husband's the snake?"

She nodded. "Sure. But not the bad guy. The snake is neutral. And, for the record, I happen to like snakes."

"Okay, but this snake just bit me in the foot. What did I do to deserve it?"

She tilted her head again, and this time her tone softened. "Maybe you scared it. Maybe you stepped too close to something it protected." She paused. "Or maybe the snake doesn't even know…At this point, Mary Katherine, does it matter?"

Her analogy lingered in my mind long after I left the office. I was replaying it over and over, dissecting it. Why was I chasing down a snake? I'd been going back to the same questions, the same moments, replaying them until they became all-consuming in my life. I'd convinced myself that if I understood why he left, maybe the wound wouldn't hurt so much, or maybe I could fix the problem.

But was my obsession with finding answers worth it if it was only bringing more pain?

Somewhere in that analogy, I started to realize that my healing wouldn't come from understanding him. It would come from understanding myself. This was about more than the pain of a failed marriage—it was about some personal accountability. It was time for me to look at my half of the relationship to understand what had gone wrong.

I had stayed, even when the signs were very clear that the marriage was over. I stayed because I had always assumed that love required sacrifice, that staying—even when it hurt—was a sign of devotion. But was that true love, or was it the same old fear that had kept me in other places where love was conditional? Dysfunctional relationships don't happen in a vacuum; I think that was what my therapist had been trying to get me to see. I brought myself *and* my shit to the table.

It was time to own 100 percent of my 50 percent, whatever that ultimately looked like.

When I looked closer, I realized that this pattern ran deeper than I'd ever been ready to acknowledge. I had a tendency to stay in places that didn't love me back, and that tendency could be traced all the way back to childhood. I'd stayed in an unloving church, holding on out of loyalty, out of some deeply ingrained belief that I wasn't worthy of love without sacrifice. A belief that had been hammered into my brain since the moment I first walked into a youth group. I was by nature an object of God's own wrath, undeserving of love, fully reliant on grace. And now, here I was, replaying the same pattern with my marriage, convinced that love of the highest form—sacrificial love—was enough to hold all things together.

And when it didn't work, when I was left all alone holding nothing but questions, I was running circles trying to piece it together. I was willing to ask every single hard question that led me to make myself smaller—but I was too scared to ask myself why I kept choosing to stay in loves that required that of me.

Why didn't I love myself enough to know when it was time to leave?

I took those big questions out of my therapist's office and carried them around in my heart. I held on to them gently, feeling their weight and their edges, knowing this was the beginning of change.

I kept hiking, but the motivation inside me had shifted. It wasn't about hoping he'd find me out there, or that the trees would somehow reveal his reasons. I began walking for me. The trail became less about escape and more about healing. And with each step, I felt a quiet accountability settling into my bones. I didn't have control over his actions, but I did have control over my own.

Each step I took became a reminder that I was responsible for my own happiness. I was no longer a passive character in someone else's story; I was the author of my own healing. I'd look up at the canopy, watch the way the light dappled through the leaves, feeling the breeze against my skin and the rhythm of my steps as they fell in line with my own heartbeat. It was as if, for the first time, I could feel the world around me with the same intensity that I felt the wound within me. Each step was a release, a small acknowledgment of the hurt, a letting-go of the questions I didn't need to chase anymore.

In the end, the snake was never going to give me what I needed. It was time to stop chasing answers and start asking myself the hard questions that would lead me to freedom. To heal, I had to let go of the fantasy of understanding him or finding closure from someone else. I had to care enough about my own pain to tend to it myself, to let the wound breathe and begin to heal and close.

And with every mile, every step on the trail, I learned to love myself enough to stop chasing down snakes. The journey was no longer about him, no longer about why he left or how he felt. Piece by piece, I found the strength to begin my own healing.

To hold my own hand through the pain.

CHAPTER 14

No Hate Like Christian Love

Tag groups make me so happy. If you don't know what a tag group is, that's fine. I'll lead the way. You see, I am what the social media world considers an elder millennial. It's a term that I qualify for; and if you're asking: No, I haven't come to terms with it yet. Was the goal of coining this term to make all of us face our mortality? Probably not, but here we are.

Back to tag groups.

Facebook is my happy place and it will remain my happy place, until it's pried from my sunspotted hands. Scrolling is basically a stim for me now, and I do it when I need to unwind. There's nothing like the comedic gold of an unhinged comments section. And an unhinged comments section is the primary ecosystem within which tag groups exist. Tag groups are just like any other group, except the name of the group is super niche—usually a joke or a hilarious thought people share. And then, it gets tagged in the comments.

For example, take some viral picture of a pelican whose eye is deadlocked on the camera. It looks like an evil professor plotting to take over the world. Everyone agrees, and the comments take off into a back-and-forth banter for greatness. And in those comments, you see a blue comment that says, "Birds with Threatening Auras." And you're like, "Hmmmm, that's funny; how super specific; how could there possibly be a group for this?"

Oooooh, but there is.

I'm also in a group called "It Is Bats." This one is particularly fun because there's no punctuation, so it can be a question: It is bats? Or a statement: It is bats!

I swear, it's the most delightful gathering.

It all started when a food blogger popped up in my news feed, bragging about some delicious chicken wings. I wanted to be happy for this woman, I did. She was so proud of her husband, who had "mastered the art of smoked BBQ wings."

If that sounds a little redundant, it is. You shouldn't have to smoke something you already barbecued, not unless it's some sort of cremation. But based on the charcoal color of this "dinner," it was clear this caption was accurate. Now, these wings weren't the kind that were tucked in tight like the little drumsticks at KFC. They were whole-ass, outstretched wings, the color of the night.

Like a plate full of bats.

I had that thought and then two seconds later, right there in the comments section was a blue tag group: It Is Bats.

I was intrigued, so I clicked through and joined the group. Every day since, my news feed has been sprinkled with posts that maaaay or may not be bats. It adds a little something to my life, and I love it.

Not all tag groups are ha-ha funny. Some of them are a little more twisted. For instance the group No Hate Like Christian Love. It comes exactly as billed. From all over the interwebs, posts pour in and evidence continues to grow, proving over and over what I've always suspected: Christians really suck at loving.

The amount of snarky "I'll pray for yous" or "You'll find out when you're in hells" or bizarro conspiracy theories about numbers that add up to 666...I could go on.

If you know, you know; if you don't, you should probably join.

If you can stomach it.

I have to admit, sometimes it's hard. I've seen things that are downright triggering. But I stay and I read and I learn, because stepping outside the Christian bubble is an important thing to do.

When you know how the "secular" world feels about us, it's hard not to stop and ask questions.

Aside from that, I ain't gonna lie—the posts can be funny as hell.

Remember my redheaded friend who was awarded Heretic of the Year? The one who fights Christian nationalism on the internet and is famous with the cool kids on TikTok?

April Ajoy, yep that's her.

She has a whole TikTok series based on the content that is found (or belongs) in that group. It's called "Things Christians Said on the Internet This Week," and it totally turns over my giggle box.

April's humor is the darkest of dark, and that's one of the reasons I love her. She thrives in the realm of religious black comedy because she is an exvangelical. One night, April and I spent the evening lying in a hotel bed like two teenagers at a slumber party, comparing trauma notes and laughing 'til our stomachs hurt.

Imagine our delight when we realized we'd both written Christian songs about September 11. I performed my original pop—yes, pop—song at the high school talent show. I was wearing red, white, and blue, because obviously. The kids seemed to love it, which doesn't mean much, because they were probably missing algebra to watch it.

But I do recall finishing the song and thinking that some of the faculty looked a little uncomfortable. At the time, I just figured the Holy Spirit was convicting them. When I didn't win, it was practically persecution. Now that I'm older, my guess is that maaaybe the bass drop was a little too much. You know, considering the subject matter and the fact that it had been like…two months.

April's song was more appropriate musically, but lyrically? Absolutely bonkers. But apparently, they were the perfect amount of bonkers for the folks at *The 700 Club* because yessir, she sang it on national television.

I about peed myself watching the video. It was hard to believe it was all real.

April and I are not the same people that we were back then, but we still very much love Jesus. We bond over the fact that we call ourselves Christians—and that the label carries serious baggage.

Like looking around at a wild family reunion and thinking, *Holy crap, everyone's crazy.* Then you look down and realize you're all wearing the same sweatshirts and suddenly it's a horrifying trip.

This journey has pulled April, me, and so many others in a million different directions. We started off on one end of the religious spectrum: Bible-thumping, proselytizing, missionaries. If our total at checkout was $6.66, you better believe we were both grabbing bubble gum.

It's funny now, but was it then?

I still have a hard time knowing.

Then we both swung in the opposite direction: untethered, unfiltered, and free. I can't speak for April, but I speak for myself when I say that phase was delightful.

From full-blown missionary to full-blown heretic, I now stand somewhere in the middle.

Which, oddly enough, has become a big problem, since America is a country where faith is wrapped up like a Twizzler with national politics. Sometimes, I feel like I'm standing in the middle of a highway where everyone is driving by angry.

Too liberal for most church folks.

Too religious for progressives.

You can imagine how that plays out on the internet, being loathed by polar extremes.

For me, this life is made all the more complicated by two conflicting personality traits. One, I am a loudmouth who has big opinions and a penchant for expressing them well. But two, I also have a very sensitive soul that registers every insult. Which means, I wholeheartedly speak from my soapbox, but as soon as the barbs start flying, I retreat into my shell, cry in my bed, and need a good bit of therapy to recover.

I've had friends suggest that I leave this work and find something else to do. But I don't think that's gonna change anything. Health-care workers, teachers, those in any sort of helping profession eventually experience compassion fatigue. When your caring gets way out ahead of your coping, it can wear you down to a nub.

Some people may call us oversensitive or a mess, and that's their valid perspective. But mine's a bit different. I fall more into the Glennon Doyle camp. She said, "You are not a mess. You're a feeling person in a messy world."

And isn't that actually the problem?

In this book you have probably already gathered that I love the LGBTQIA community. That's a soapbox I step up to as often as my resilience will allow. What I see in the alphabet mafia is exactly what I see and love about Jesus. Facing deep hatred from people who don't get it, these folks double down on love. They love freely, extravagantly, and courageously every day. That there shows a whole lot of heart.

So, despite the pitchforks showing up to my page, I continue to make posts about my alphabet family, especially as it pertains to church.

NOT THAT WHEEL, JESUS!

(When I say family, I mean A as in ally. Sorry to disappoint.)

I made one such post after being inspired by a trending sound on TikTok. It was a ten-second clip from the new Willy Wonka film, cut from a catchy little song.

"Oompa loompa doopity doo; I've got a baaaad feeling 'bout you."

In order to jump on a TikTok trend, here's what you're supposed to do: Take a sound and use it in a way that is unique to you (or your niche). Someone with IBS might show themselves ordering a burrito from Taco Bell.

Get it?

Anyways, I immediately knew what my take was gonna be. The caption was simply this:

> POV: wrote the church an email asking if they are
> affirming & the pastor replies asking me to coffee.

To be fair, I have personal experience on both sides of that Starbucks table, and it was terrible from every seat. Never mind the whole point of asking this question was to avoid this exact kind of runaround. Any pastor who dodges a direct theological question gets the oompa loompa song from now on.

I got a baaaaad feeling 'bout you.

I laughed and I posted that video, which brought out all the typical stuff. A few unfollows, a bunch of confused readers. Some people loved it, some people hated it; it was split about fifty-fifty. But there was quite a Venn diagram overlap of folks who believed this was my coming-out party. Maybe, because of my unexpected divorce, this offered them some explanation. But this assumption was a wrong one, and holy crap did it kick an anthill. The comments exploded into a mixed bag of congratulations and condemnation.

This unintended insinuation landed my content into some dark corner of a Reddit rabbit hole, which activated a whole freaking army of basement-dwelling keyboard warriors. They converged on my page, unified in one purpose—not arguing Scripture, not sharing their truth, but quite simply: to tear me down.

"No wonder your husband left, you're a lesbo."

"Of course any godly man would leave this idiot. I hope he finds someone smarter and prettier."

"When you're burning in hell, you'll see the truth."

I was fragile that week. It hit me hard. And like a cornered animal, I lashed out. I doubled down in the content, which meant double the attacks, and the math only snowballed from there.

I fought fire with fire, Scripture with Scripture. I was delivering knockouts in the comments. I can cite the Hebrew, Aramaic, and Greek. I have *Strong's Exhaustive Concordance* in my library. I knew their arguments before they were typed, and I had strategies to overcome all of them. The truth is, I had gotten so good at this ridiculous game that I could fight and win for both sides. I guess that's what happens when you've met eight jillion pastors for a "cup of coffee" to discuss the issue.

Eventually, the fighting made me feel weary. So I turned off the comments for a while. But still, I couldn't shake this unsettling feeling that kept creeping up into my chest. Maybe I was being a big, fat hypocrite. Maybe I was cherry-picking Scripture to fight off perspectives that were built off of cherry-picked Scripture. Maybe, in my efforts to right the ship, I'd turned into the opposite extreme.

Wasn't this what those other folks did?

The ones that I'd lost all respect for?

CHAPTER 15

Good Guys and Bad Guys

I have never gone home for a high school reunion. I probably never will. Not because my hometown is some horrible place that I need to escape forever. Honestly, you can blame it on Zuckerberg. The truth is, I've been able to keep in touch with the people I care about most. I don't really have to wait ten or fifteen years to see how precious my classmates' kids are; I get to do that every day. Something happens to your news feed when you hit your late thirties—you see more pictures of your friends' kids' activities than you do of your actual friends. Not that I'm complaining. Nothing makes my heart go pitter-pat like some chubby-cheeked kids playing T-ball.

I'm grateful to be growing up in a time when that buddy who might have slipped away without the digital age gets to stick around. It's such a delight to see their arcs develop over time. As a writer, maybe that's what I love the most: watching these stories get written.

For instance, my friend Chase has an arc that's been incredible to witness. This is a guy who got picked on in math class and now he's an FBI agent. Some might call that a serious glow-up, but the thing is, Chase never changed. He's still the exact same sweet-hearted, relatable, shaggy-haired Chase. It's just that now he speaks three languages, knows hand-to-hand combat, and can disarm an assailant in seconds. Basically, every John Krasinski character ever, all rolled into one.

I had the opportunity to grab lunch with Chase a couple of years ago. I was visiting my mom in Washington, DC, and he was starting a second phase of his career after serving in the war on terror. Before this, he served in the military as some sort of interrogation specialist.

Apparently, Chase had a knack for getting into the brain of his enemy. So, when he came back home, Uncle Sam asked if Chase wanted to put those skills to new use. He was offered a role in counterterrorism. Technically, it was still the same job. But this time, he wouldn't have access to the bad guy. He'd have to think like one, instead.

America needed someone to get ahead of the problem. To stop terrorists before they could strike. Seeing a chance to make a difference, Chase accepted the job.

He worked counterterrorism for a couple of years and was thriving in his new position, even stopping at least one attack on

American soil. Occasionally, he would wind up on the stand in a courtroom to help the government lock up the bad guy. You know on *Law & Order* when they bring in an expert to testify, and that guy will sink or float a case based on their specialized knowledge? Chase was that guy for the United States—the big gun Uncle Sam would pull out in court when it was time to convince the jury.

During one such trial, Chase was brought to the stand and questioned about a terrorist he'd been tracking for years. The goal was to use this information and put a man away for life.

But Chase found himself struggling with answers because that wasn't at all what he wanted. This man, who had just turned eighteen, was clearly broken and dangerous. But when Chase had gotten into the mind of his enemy, he found that he was able to understand him—not justify what he had planned, but understand how he got there.

Still, he did his job and watched as the prosecutor, a man with the skill of a shark, asked question after careful question to set up his killer blow, painting this barely adult as a madman, a bloodthirsty demon, and an inevitable, permanent danger to society. Chase knew this was all part of the justice system. He was playing his role in the game, and the prosecutor was playing his. But then, suddenly, the eighteen-year-old's shoulders started shaking.

He said something—just one word—that Chase recognized in Arabic.

"Ummi."

The boy was crying for his mother.

The young man, sitting there accused of planning terror, wanted his mother. He wanted her comfort, her presence, but she no longer existed. And in that moment, Chase no longer felt the clarity he'd had when he walked into the courtroom that day. He saw not a monster, but a child who had been swallowed by grief and anger, lost in a world that had offered him nothing but pain.

Chase could feel the jury watching him, waiting for his testimony to bring the hammer down. But instead, he hesitated, a crack forming in the confidence he had carried to the stand. That hesitation spoke volumes, even in a room where silence was supposed to mean agreement.

Yes, this man was dangerous. Yes, he had done terrible things. But Chase had come to understand why. He saw how this man had been a child once, growing up in poverty, his family killed in war, his life full of pain and anger. Chase understood because he'd felt that same rage when he lost his own friend and fellow soldier.

That's when Chase looked at me and said something that's stayed with me ever since: "Maybe the difference between good guys and bad guys is simply who narrates the story."

His words struck a chord. I wasn't sure it was that black-and-white, but I couldn't stop chewing on the idea. Was it possible that I was the bad guy in somebody else's story? Perhaps, even a part of my own? That thought stopped me in my tracks. I had felt like a victim for so long, and that was valid, but...who had I hurt?

The concept of radical accountability had been touched on by my therapist in the past, and I was becoming very eager to explore it. What was it that my therapist told me? To stop chasing snakes and own 100 percent of my 50 percent?

That was all well and good as a colloquialism, but what did it mean in my life? Where do you even start shadow work—and what is its practical application?

With all of these questions tumbling around in my head, I turned to a friend who I knew would have answers, someone whose life I knew to be a powerful example of this good guy and bad guy duality.

Six years sober, Matt is a recovered alcoholic, raising four teenagers on his own. Their mother, Rachel, also struggled with addiction, tragically passing away from an accidental overdose. Her radiant joy and beautiful voice brought light into the lives of those around her, and her untimely death robbed the world of that sunshine—a loss deeply felt by all who knew her.

She died in bed while the children were home, and they had been the ones to discover her body. His oldest daughter, Caroline, had even tried to save her, administering CPR as a thirteen-year-old.

Almost immediately after their mother's passing, the children moved in with their dad, changing cities and schools—a massive, traumatic shift in the middle of an already destabilizing moment.

When I think of that point in their family story, it feels unfathomable to me. Their worlds were completely upended and now they were sleeping in unfamiliar beds. Their mother's absence could be felt in the walls of the house, a void they couldn't escape. And there was Matt—newly sober and deeply determined—trying to steady their lives when everything had just fallen apart. There's no map for navigating that kind of loss, and trauma like that leaves unavoidable scars—you might even wonder if it's possible to overcome. I certainly did when I first heard their story. But somehow, Matt's home healed into a place of incredible safety and love, and his teenagers are the epitome of joy.

I remember the first time I met his family, I was shocked by their open dialogue, loving rapport, and, frankly, their dark brand of humor. They don't shy away from the trauma that ripped them to pieces—they hold it close. They examine it, cry over it, and, somehow, they laugh about it, too.

One example sticks with me: Their school was having a spirit day where everyone wore a white T-shirt, and on it was written a "white lie." Things like "My dad is president" or "I ran 10 miles this morning." One of the oldest kids, whose wit is sharp and quick, simply wrote, "My mom made me breakfast."

When I tell you I was floored—I mean, I couldn't respond or wrap my mind around this sort of humor. But it works for them. It's how they've made peace with their pain, how they've woven it into their lives instead of letting it consume them. It's their way of reclaiming control over something uncontrollable.

What struck me most, though, was how much they truly love and support one another. It's evident in the way they tease each other, always with affection, almost never with malice. They've found a way to keep their family close-knit, leaning on each other in ways that make their bond almost tangible. The laughter in their house doesn't hide the pain—it heals it. There's a kind of magic in the way they've turned tragedy into connection.

Matt, as their father, has created this culture. He speaks about his past with honesty, acknowledging the duality of all of it—the beauty and the pain, the love and the failures. And he has to, because the reality is stark: Both he and the children's mother failed those kids for a period of time. Addiction robbed them of the parents they deserved. But there are also beautiful memories to honor, moments of love and connection that still matter.

It took a lot of work for Matt to see that duality. To look back on his life and hold both truths at once—the harm and the healing, the mistakes and the grace. And that's why I reached out to him. Because he knew, in a way I was just beginning to understand, that what Chase said was true.

I've always been told that you shouldn't seek advice from people whose lives you wouldn't want to emulate. If someone has a messy marriage, they're probably not the person you should call for relationship advice. And while I wouldn't want to replicate Matt's trauma or the experiences that brought him to this point, the healing he had found—the calm, honest, and resilient home he had built—was something I deeply desired for myself. He might not be an expert at many things, but at healing the man has some wisdom.

So, when I reached out to tell Matt I felt stuck in my healing—so angry at the church and hurt by my marriage—it didn't take too much information for him to know exactly what I meant. He understood that I was carrying that pain like a burden

I couldn't put down, and it was running my life. Without hesitation, he reached for his battered copy of *Alcoholics Anonymous*, a book so worn and marked with notes and highlighter that it looked like a well-loved Bible.

He flipped it open, right to the section he wanted, as if he knew exactly what I needed to hear. He didn't have to search for the words—they were already waiting for me, the kind of truth that comes only from living it.

"Resentment," he read, his voice steady and sure, and the word hit me square in the chest. For a moment, I froze. It felt like he'd been reading my mail. Not the paper letters, but the kind in your heart—the writing of my internal dialogue. All the anger I had carried, the bitterness I thought I had hidden, was apparently glaringly transparent to Matt.

Sure, I had expressed some frustration to my friend, but resentment?

That's a hell of a word.

And I knew right away it was an accurate one. Matt wasn't accusing me—he was offering me a lifeline, one that I hadn't even realized I needed. He was peeling back the layers of my heart, exposing the root of what I'd been struggling with.

"Resentment shuts us off from the sunlight of the spirit," he continued. "For us, holding on to anger is fatal. If we want to live, we have to be free of it."

That phrase—sunlight of the spirit—stuck with me. It evoked a brightness I hadn't felt in years. It reminded me of the person I used to be, the one people once described as full of sunshine and joy. But that was before the anger, before I went nuclear on social media, railing against the church and the people who had hurt me. I could still recall the shock in my audience's responses: "You? You're always so positive. So joyful."

They couldn't reconcile the girl they knew with the person I had become—always angry, always kicking up dirt.

But I could. I knew exactly what had happened. A dark cloud had formed over my injured spirit, and I'd let it linger there for far too long. Hearing Matt say those words made me realize just how heavy that cloud had become, how much light it had stolen from me. It wasn't much, just a few words from a book, but he was right—the resentment was killing me. It had wrecked more than just my faith or my marriage—it had wrecked me. While I had truly been a victim of many people and circumstances, I was living in that role so fully that I felt no agency over anything happening in my life. And I resented all of it. I was furious—furious that I had been a victim, furious at the people who had hurt me, furious that no one seemed to care. The rage had consumed me, leaving no space for anything else.

All this anger was shutting me off from the sunlight I used to live in, and I couldn't keep going like this.

Matt could see it in my eyes. The searching. I didn't even have to say it out loud. I wanted to know the way forward, but I was terrified of what the answer might be.

"Forgiveness," he said gently, and I bristled immediately. That word was exactly what I feared. My mind flashed to that Christian counselor from so many years ago, telling me to forgive without any acknowledgment of the harm I'd suffered. My walls went up so fast I could almost hear the doors slamming shut.

But Matt saw that, too. Instead, he leaned in and continued. "Forgiveness doesn't negate accountability," he said, holding my gaze. "It just means you let go of the anger that's holding you back. Some people might never apologize to you, and that's on them. But you can clean up your side of the street."

I could feel the weight of his words settling over me. This wasn't blind forgiveness or forced reconciliation. This was about reclaiming the parts of my life that resentment had stolen, about finding agency where I had seen only pain. And Matt knew that struggle because he had walked it himself. He had found rock bottom, lived there too long, and finally climbed his way out.

So I asked him the question that was heavy in my mind, one that made this formula seem impossible.

"Do you resent her? The mother of your children? For the chaos her addiction caused, for what the kids are still healing from?"

Immediately, he shook his head no. "For a while, yes. But I made amends with her before she died," he said. His voice was calm and weighted with meaning. "I apologized for my part in it—the chaos, the destruction of our marriage. I owned all of my side of the story."

I sat there, trying to wrap my mind around it. I knew account-ability was important, sure. "But…how?" I asked. "How do you get to that place? How do you forgive someone for everything they've done, especially when they aren't even sorry?"

Matt paused, looking at me with the kind of clarity that only comes from hard-earned wisdom. "Because I was sick, Mary Katherine," he said. "That's what I had to face. All the harm I caused—the lies, the chaos, the destruction—it was because I was sick. Addiction isn't just physical. It's spiritual. And once I could see that about myself, it wasn't hard to see it in her."

The truth of those words was heavy and undeniable. I took a breath to let it all soak in. He went on, "Anybody behaving that way is sick. It's a spiritual sickness, and it breaks people. It often breaks families. But when I looked at her through that lens, I couldn't hate her anymore. I couldn't even resent her. She needed the same grace I needed."

And that's when something clicked for me.

The harm I'd endured, the betrayal and the wounds that had shaped my life—they had come from sick people. It wasn't about excusing them or forgetting what they'd done. It was about understanding that their actions weren't born out of strength, but weakness. They were broken, just as I had been in my own ways.

And just as I am, in some ways, still.

Early in my deconstruction journey, I cast myself as the hero. I held on to that notion for a long time, seeing myself as the maligned, heart of gold champion, come to save the uninformed from themselves. But I would be a huge freaking hypocrite to get to this place in my journey where I'm holding the bad guys accountable, only to conveniently dodge the fact that my name is on that list.

I know that I've hurt people. I'm certain I have. In somebody else's journey, I have been the bad guy. Real and lasting harm had been done to me by the church and I was passing it on like a good soldier. Under the banner of that holy mission, I became somewhat of a Crusader.

And despite what the Christian school cheerleaders said, it's not "great to be" one.

Which leads me to here.

I've been a Crusader in the name of the church and I've been a Crusader in the name of deconstruction and here's the deal: Those roles have made me the good guy in some stories and the bad guy in others, depending on the story you're telling yourself.

Here's what I know for sure: Yes, I've been hurt. And I've also hurt people all along the way. Yes, my ex-husband did things that caused our marriage to fall apart. But so did I.

And the only way I know for any of us to start untangling our pain and fear and trauma is to apologize for all the things we've done in the name of Jesus and in reaction to what was done to us in the name of Jesus. And once my perspective was humbled by this realization, I knew what I needed to do.

The first step was reaching out to my ex-husband. I didn't need him to acknowledge his part in the breakdown of our marriage, because this wasn't about him. It was about me letting go of the resentment I had carried for so long. When we spoke, I told him I was sorry—sorry for my financial illiteracy and the ways it caused strain, sorry for being ashamed and hiding things from him. I apologized for pressuring him to get married so young, for using the church as a justification for something we weren't ready for. It didn't matter that I believed those things back then; they had caused harm to our relationship, and that was on me.

As I owned my side of things, I felt a release I hadn't anticipated. It wasn't just about the apology—it was about the freedom that came with letting something go. This, I realized, was my path forward. "Forgive us our debts, as we forgive our debtors."

The next day, I sat down to write more apologies. The healing I found was addicting. This was the work I needed to do, and I knew I'd be doing it for quite some time. But getting started felt like the most important thing, and the words flowed out of me like water.

As I wrote, the dark cloud that had hung over me for so long began to lift, almost immediately. It wasn't just a metaphor—I could feel the sunlight of my soul returning, just as Matt had told me it would. With every apology, every act of accountability, I felt a weight lifting. For the first time in years, I was starting to feel peace.

Here are a few of my apologies:

To Amy, whom I told about the Rapture in nightmarish detail at the tender age of eleven: I'm sorry I ruined your slumber party by trying to save your soul. I'm sorry I told you that any minute your parents could just disappear, and planes would start falling from the sky, and Satan would take over the planet. I was taught that your salvation was my responsibility, and that was a lot for a kid. But I understand now why we never hung out after that, and I'm so, so sorry.

To Christine, my classmate at Carver Middle School: We talked about church at the lunch table. I remember you were eating a Pizza Lunchable when you told me your family was Catholic. You tried to educate me about your beliefs, but I argued that you weren't a Christian. We fought, you cried, and we never spoke again. If you remember me, please know I am sorry.

To Becca, my precious friend who bravely shared that she thought she might be gay during a Bible study: I'm sorry for how I responded, saying I'd "love you no matter what" and pray for clarity. To insinuate that your identity was something to be overcome was both wrong and hurtful. You are fearfully and wonderfully made, my friend, and I'm sorry it took you so long to hear that from me. Your presence in my life is a gift of grace. I'm sorry it took me so long to truly see you.

To Chris from the varsity football team, who asked me out to dinner: I am sorry I said God wanted me to be single. He clearly said no such thing; I was just a coward who didn't know how to politely turn down an invitation. That was a cop-out, and a hurtful one. I learned that nasty trick when I was dumped by a Presbyterian pastor's kid. For what it's worth, I'm truly sorry, especially since I knew how awful it felt.

To Thailand, where I served as a missionary: I loved you with a sincere heart, but I'm sorry I acted as if the Thai people needed answers from someone like me. The truth was actually the opposite. Living in Thailand was a sacred experience, and I was privileged to learn from your culture. My intentions might have been pure, but my message was certainly not. I brought a tourism gospel and a colonizing gaze to a people who were asking for neither.

I am sorry for my arrogance, my self-righteous spirit, and my failure to love you well.

To my brother, Ty: I am sorry I begged Dad to make you attend that intense youth group event. You were totally right—it was culty. I should have respected your boundaries. Thank you for loving me through all my phases: the new theologies, the revivals, the insistence that "YOU HAVE TO COME THIS SUNDAY; IT'S SUCH AN IMPORTANT MESSAGE." The message was fine, and you were fine to miss it.

To every old person at the nursing home in Dothan, Alabama: Oh, Lord, I am sorry. There are no words sufficient for the crimes I committed in God's very own waiting room. I am sorry for singing the Batman verse of "Jingle Bells" during the Christmas trip. I'm sorry for drawing a pooping dog on your card from the fifth-grade Sunday school class. And I am sincerely sorry for asking if you had let Jesus into your heart, with the very heavy insinuation that you might soon meet Him. So, if you remember me—the knock-kneed, ponytailed girl who asked if you'd ever met Jesus—please know I am truly sorry for treating you like a "pound puppy with an Adopt-By date."

To every classmate whose yearbook I signed with "Philippians 4:13!!!" I'm sorry. That was over the top, super churchy, and I hope you had a really great summer anyway.

To the audience of the high school talent show that had to listen to my original "Christian" song about 9/11 just two months after it happened: You weren't crazy; it was way too soon, and the bass was a bit much for the content. Sorry I sucker punched you all with that cringeworthy performance. Thanks for not laughing me offstage. Also, sorry I acted shocked when I didn't win. And I'm even more sorry for assuming I lost because "y'all hated Jesus." I never said it out loud, but I thought it. And that's bad enough to merit a confession.

To the LGBTQIA community, nonbelievers, and anyone else I hurt by wielding an unloving gospel: I am sorry you were made to feel unwelcome. I'm sorry you were lied to. I'm sorry for the heartache, trauma, and oppression you experienced in the name of Jesus. God is love, and love shouldn't hurt. It sure as hell shouldn't leave scars. But for far too long, and for far too many, that's exactly what church has become: an injury. I am sorry for the role I played in that trauma.

I am sorry, so sorry, to anyone I hurt by wielding an unloving gospel. My queer friends, my friends of differing faiths, my friends who were not believers.

To anyone who flinches at the hand of the church, I am sorry for the role I played in that trauma.

Which brings me to my final apology, to the person I injured most. Whose childlike faith was chewed to bits in the jaws of an angry church.

To myself.

I am sorry we didn't get out sooner.

I wish so badly I could reach back in time to hug you and offer some comfort. Things got worse before you finally left. You should never have been in that position.

I cannot help but think back to all those years ago, when

you first walked into a church—not because your parents were driving, but because you were excited to be there. You wanted to know God and have fellowship with His people. You were looking for love and community. But the child that walked into that church was not the same one that came out. You walked through those doors with hope for healing and came limping out, hurt and afraid. Afraid of hell, of other Christians…afraid of even your own faith.

For that, I am truly sorry.

I am sorry for all the times you felt pressure to be perfect, pure, and obedient. I am sorry for the teachings of Purity Culture that made you question your worth. I am sorry for the patriarchal culture that taught you to distrust your instincts.

I am sorry for every oppressive ritual that required your participation. I'm sorry your sense of agency was lost in the name of "godly submission."

I'm sorry damnation was used as a tool to control and manipulate you. I'm sorry you were convinced that tool was useful for the reaching and teaching of others.

I am sorry that the pastor you trusted so much turned out to be such a big jerk. I'm sorry he spiked the punch bowl of church with those nasty, divisive politics. I am sorry you heard it, sorry you believed it, sorry you had to leave.

I'm sorry that leaving was made so hard by other gaslighting, hurtful believers.

I am sorry the church failed when you needed support. That you were judged and rarely shown grace. I'm sorry that instead of inclusion and love, you were thrown into distrust and chaos. I am sorry you suffered from abuse in church, and that the church covered up that abuse. I am sorry you learned that your body was a problem, and your nature was inherently evil. I'm sorry for the self-loathing, self-sacrificing things you tried in the search for atonement.

And I'm sorry that when the church broke our heart, we blamed those injuries on Jesus.

Jesus, the very embodiment of love, compassion, forgiveness, and grace. Jesus, the Shepherd of every lost soul. Who never abandoned His sheep. Jesus was standing there all along, wanting our broken pieces.

I'm sorry for listening to the accusers. For letting the gate-keepers in. Their barbs cut deep, my anger grew, and those wounds began to fester.

I'm sorry that instead of healing, my church hurt, I let it behind the wheel.

Hurt was a really bad driver.

Looking back, I see a journey that has been far from perfect but has brought me closer to the person I want to be. I understand that true healing isn't about forgetting what's happened but about facing it with clear eyes, owning my part, and letting grace guide the rest.

Through this process, I learned something profound: Sometimes we're the hero in our story, sometimes the villain, and most of the time, we're just...people. Fallible, hurt, and hurting. The truth about "bad guys" and "good guys" is that most of the time, we're both. If we can see that—really see it—we might just find the peace we've been looking for all along.

CHAPTER 16

Word of God

Since childhood, I've had a spiritual itchiness about the way we interpret Scripture. I suspected the adults around me were just winging it, and that suspicion only grew as I lobbed question after question at my wide-eyed Sunday school teachers.

Why would God say it's okay to have slaves?

Why did God send a bear to kill a whole freaking town because two kids mocked a preacher's bald head? Talk about overkill. And this is the God I'm supposed to trust? My loving, heavenly Father?

What about the Flood? Good for Noah and all…but to be clear, God drowned the whole planet?

But I was shhh'ed and head-patted and told to have faith. Because the Word of God was inerrant and infallible. If I prayed and had faith and was a good little Christian, its meaning would eventually become clear.

The lesson, of course, was that all of my questioning came down to my own broken nature. If the Bible wasn't clear, it was because my heart was deceiving me. So, I kept trying to get right with the Lord.

I got baptized and baptized again and again, as if I could waterboard the sinful nature out of me. I fasted. I prayed and listened for God's voice. Then got in arguments in my own head over who was actually responding.

Is that You, God?

No, it's still us, Mary Katherine.

Hold on, self; that doesn't make sense. Why would I answer my own prayers?

Oh no—is this Satan playing a trick?

GET THEE BEHIND ME, SATAN!

GOD, are You there?

No, it's me, Satan.

Shut up, self; that isn't funny.

I read the Word of God forward and backward, I preached it in the 10/40 Window. I did Bible studies, bought all sorts of handbooks, and waited for the Bible to become clear.

But for me, after all those years of effort—Scripture remained clear as mud.

I internalized this failure to find biblical clarity, and it caused me to question so much. Those questions didn't simply extend to theology; they extended to myself as a human. Was I the problem? Incapable of understanding? Had I hardened my heart beyond repair? Was I so deeply sinful and lost in my own turmoil that I was no longer able to see truth? Or had God simply made me to be one of those people who were destined for eternal torment? The flip side of grace, after all, is condemnation. You don't need saving if there's nothing to be saved from. Maybe I was sent here to become an example of "what not to do" for the saved ones.

I was good with Jesus. It was Scripture I most often had trouble with. My inability to reconcile Scripture with Jesus was the most devastating rip to my faith sweater. No matter how hard I tried, I just couldn't believe every word of the Bible was to be taken literally. But then there was Jesus, this Rabbi I adored—whose teachings undeniably changed me. He existed within the mass of those whisper-thin pages, and His words struck me straight in the heart.

Was I allowed to follow Christ and question the Bible? Was it possible to simultaneously, wholeheartedly believe in His teachings while questioning the pages that held them?

· · · · · · · · · ·

Once upon a time in a land far away (assuming you don't live in Palestine), a baby was born in a manger and His name was Joshua.

Technically, his Hebrew name was Yeshua, which directly translates to Joshua, but that's not what happened for whatever reason, and now we all know Him as Jesus.

It would be a mess to start changing the hymn lyrics now, and, frankly, I can't imagine blessing someone in Josh's name. So, for accuracy's sake, I'm sharing the backstory; but for continuity—let's stick with Jesus.

Jesus grew up in a Jewish household, and He was a very special child. According to apocryphal writings (confirmed as authentic, but not in the Bible), five-year-old Jesus once went to a river during the Sabbath to play in the mud. He molded twelve sparrows from the riverbank clay, and when the religious leaders saw this, they went straight to Joseph to shame his parenting, because his kid had "profaned" the Sabbath. So Joseph marched his frustrated butt to the river where, indeed, little Jesus was playing. And he cried out (I'll paraphrase), "Duuuuude. What are You doing? Don't You know this is breaking the Law?"

To which Little Kid Jesus clapped and said, "Be gone!" and the clay turned into actual birds. The gathered crowd was shocked by this spectacle, so they went to go tell the whole town. And at this point, I am certain, Joseph pinched the bridge of his nose, like "What am I gonna do with this kid?"

Parenthood never got easier for Joseph. Because while Jesus was destined for greatness, every move He made on that journey was perceived as an affront by the religious establishment.

As a Jew, there was a path for Jesus to follow if He wanted to become a religious leader. And some scholars believe He took that path. That the Jewish leaders saw how brilliant Jesus was and enrolled Him in a school for rabbis. While this would account for the eighteen years of His life that are missing from canonical

Scripture, I have a hard time reconciling the idea that this rebel was institutionally educated.

Either way, according to the Gospel of Luke, that time in His life was well spent: "Jesus increased in wisdom and stature, and in favor with God and man" (2:52 KJV).

Regardless of whether He was formally educated, Jesus became known as a Rabbi. He lived by Jewish law, spoke about Jewish law, and He was referred to as the "King of the Jews" at the beginning of His life and at the end.

My point is, regardless of what you believe about the Man, there is one thing that really can't be argued. Jesus was super, duper Jewish. As Christians, we often forget that.

But the thing is, if you reeeeally want to know somebody—you must first understand their culture.

. . . .

After failing out of college and finding Jesus for the second (or third?) time, I got invited to attend a Passion conference, headed by Beth Moore and Louie Giglio. While we were there, a beautiful worship song was playing, and everyone bowed their heads to pray. The speaker asked if anyone was feeling the Spirit lead them to become a missionary. I wasn't sure if it was the Spirit or if I was in my own head, but there was definitely a still, small voice whispering to me that I should go; this was what God would want from me. Maybe God would have wanted me to study in school, or stay home and make a little money, or just learn to be an adult—I dunno—but that's not what the voice was saying. It was saying, "Go overseas; the whole world needs you."

And so, obviously, I answered that call. I went to the tent where all the newly called missionaries were supposed to sign up for our service (pretty epic how they knew someone was going to be called and had sign-up sheets ready to go; how neat). When asked specifically where God was calling me to go, I was offered a brochure of options along with pictures and summaries beside each country name. It felt like some weird, holy game of MASH. Where will you end up? Where will YOU teach the gospel? I ended up choosing Thailand, for reasons that are still entirely unclear to me, but at the time, it all felt very holy. And in my first week of spreading this mission overseas, I was in for a bit of a culture shock.

My first day as a teacher in Thailand, I barged into class with my hands full. I had a purse, a bunch of books, some craft supplies that I'd purchased, and about eighteen zillion posters. At some point, a poster slipped out of the pile, landing propped up against a wall.

"Can you help me with that?" I asked my assistant, but she didn't see what I was talking about. My hands were still full, so I used my foot to point out where the poster had landed.

"Riiiight there," I emphasized once again, pointing my foot to direct her.

At this point, there were probably ten students sitting in desks, and I could hear a collective gasp. You see, in Asia, pointing your foot at something is deeply, deeply offensive. And I wasn't just pointing my foot at a poster—it was a poster of the King of Thailand.

Thank God, that gasp was followed by giggles. The uncomfortable kind, but still. They had grace for my ignorance, which was nice because I'd learn later that I could've been arrested for less. Disrespecting the king is no joke in Thailand. Many Americans learn that the hard way. And this is why cultural context matters. It changes the meaning of everything.

My children attended a Jewish preschool, and I'm grateful for that every day. We chose Temple Judea because it was safe and small with a reasonable tuition schedule. What we didn't plan for was the cultural learning—which turned out to be the best part.

Each Friday, the kids would celebrate Shabbat, and on the holidays, they were taught about Jewish customs. I'll never forget my piggy-tailed Holland coming home with a grin on her face, telling me all about the upcoming holiday and how she was going to celebrate:

"We'll light candles, eat latkes, and make dreidels together. And we all say 'Honey Cup Sameach'!"

"…Oh, that's nice…What does it mean?"

"It means 'Haaaaaappy Honey Cup'!"

To be honest, it took me enough of a minute that I decided to pop into the preschool and ask the director how my family should prepare for this upcoming Honey Cup season.

Joanne is a very regal woman, but when I asked her she cackled loudly. And she didn't stop, either, for at least thirty seconds. She was slapping her thighs and everything. Finally, when she regained her composure, she asked me to take a seat. Then she spent the next little while teaching a clueless Christian about Hanukkah.

Leaving Joanne's office, I was hit with a wave of liberal guilt. It was occurring to me that the majority of families at her school weren't members of the synagogue. Which meant, more than likely, she spent a lot of her time explaining Jewish traditions.

"Joanne," I said, stepping back through the door. "I'm sorry I took so much time. I hadn't considered the fact that you probably get asked a million questions like this in a week."

"Please," Joanne laughed, leaning back in her chair. "To be Jewish is to ask questions."

· · · · · · · · · ·

Remember how I told you about Usher on roller skates at the Taylor Swift Super Bowl show? I was the exact target audience for this content, but I wasn't tuning in to see Usher. My hopes were high that a certain hype man might be joining his buddy onstage. And when I heard "YeaaaAAaaah," I came up off my seat before transporting straight back to college.

If I look hard enough through the Jägermeister haze, I can see us at Tiki Bob's. Wearing cheesy ribbon belts and dancing in ways that resembled some mating ritual. And there is Lil Jon, the indisputable king of hype, yeah-ing us all through the night.

Everyone needs a friend like Lil Jon.

Even an ancient Rabbi.

Imagine my excitement when I was reading through Scripture and discovered that Jesus had a hype man. Not only that, his name was John. This John didn't exactly yell "Yeah" behind Christ, but he did make a rad introduction. And getting the crowd hyped up for the show is honestly half the battle. In this case, the "show" was the gospel of Christ, and John wanted everyone to hear it. The stories and words of Jesus are coming, and readers anticipate that. But first, John gets out in front of those readers and offers this epic intro: "In the beginning was the Word, and the Word was with God, and the Word was God. He was with God in the beginning" (John 1:1–2).

Don't womp womp me. I know this isn't the kind of intro that sends a pop star to the Super Bowl in roller skates…but in the cultural context of biblical times, this statement was a bomb of meaning.

John was announcing to anyone who would listen that the Word of God wasn't a book—but a being that was there in the beginning. Not laws. Not directives. Not an exclusive guest list of who can and can't go to heaven.

A person.

And not just any person.

"Listen up. This guy is the Word," John announced, before unloading the gospel of Jesus.

And it was this tiny verse, this small introduction, that caused me to slam on the brakes recently. Because—wait a minute.

If Jesus is the Word of God, what does that make the Bible? Could it be that this book, which I clung to so tightly, was intended to serve as a vessel? A library of documents containing all the stories that framed up the ministry of Jesus? What if Scripture wasn't a book of directives, but a Bible of cultural context?

Because if it was that simple...if the Word of God was Jesus... then, maybe this all did make sense. Maybe I'd missed the forest for the trees and the truth wasn't so dang complicated.

As I rolled this idea around in my heart, it felt like a sigh of relief.

The early Christian church had existed for a century or more without a canonized version of Scripture. It thrived and it grew because the believers had faith in Christ's teachings—and loved one another well.

The more I thought about it, my experience as a homeless heretic looked a lot like the early church. A bunch of broken souls communing over a belief in the gospel of Jesus, wrestling with theology and the mysteries of God, and loving one another through it.

It all felt so true...but was it allowed?

I wasn't sure who I should ask.

But I knew this: Biblical literalism was the final tile that had fallen for me. My messed-up picture of Jesus was gone, and in its place was a clean slate.

Perhaps this was the moment I stopped deconstructing. When I turned the steering wheel, just a bit, and my car ended up back on pavement. Headed—if not in the right direction, at least out of the ditch.

There was nothing left to take down. This was the moment I'd lost my whole sweater, saw the bare-naked truth, and adored it.

Last year, I received a text from a friend who just couldn't contain her excitement. First came a meme of Eminem singing, "Guess who's back, back again." Immediately after, she dropped a link to a local news story. It was a press release from First Baptist Church in Huntsville.

Eggbeater Jesus was back.

Pastor Travis was excited to share the good news, saying, "It's the same design just with different, more sturdy material. The colors are more vibrant. It's been compared to going from a standard def to high definition on television."

High. Def. Jesus.

I couldn't contain my excitement. I hopped in the car and drove straight to the church to see this with my own two eyes. And let me just say, He did not disappoint. Eggbeater Jesus was brilliant. The colors were more vibrant, the glass more translucent. He had a little shimmer in the sunlight. This update was truly an upgrade.

The revamp had been announced forever ago, but I suppose these things take time. After all, there were 1.4 million pieces to take off the wall, and 6.0 million to put back up.

Tweezer by tweezer, square by square, the process took seven years.

But here He was. Glittering in the cosmos.

A beautiful reconstruction.

CHAPTER 17

As Yourself

I didn't stop believing in Santa until my freshman year of college.

That probably tells you a whole lot about me that my therapist hasn't even touched. As we've already discussed, I'm an expert at suspending disbelief. In my logical brain, sure, I knew it was fake. I'd even caught my mom hanging a stocking. But every year, on December 24, I'd delete all that evidence from my brain. I'd crawl into bed and close my eyes tight and listen for hooves on the rooftop.

I suppose there's something deep inside me still clinging to the magic of childhood. So much of that innocence was stolen from me, and I've been trying to recover it since. That being said, it is probably unsurprising that I'm also a Disney Adult. It's a thing, and for the most part, people find us annoying. Whatever, I couldn't care less.

Disney is magical, and magic makes me happy (I say, while straightening my Minnie ears).

According to *Urban Dictionary*, a Disney Adult is "an eccentric or theatrical person who is often overly positive and lacks the self-awareness to know when people find them disruptive, or annoying."

First of all, guilty, guilty, and guilty. But that wasn't all it said. *Urban Dictionary* wasn't done with me yet, 'cause it still had a plural form.

"A group of Disney Adults is known as an Amber Alert."

Shots fired, *Urban Dictionary*. That hurt.

Still, I have a lifelong Disney obsession that only deepened when we moved to Orlando. At this point, Ben and Holland were in preschool, which meant we could play hooky anytime we wanted. So I bought annual passes, and a few times a month, that's exactly what we did. Armed to the teeth with Uncrustables and sunscreen, I'd strap my two kids into their car seats, and instead of turning left toward Bright Horizons, I'd turn right toward Interstate 4. Sometimes the kids wouldn't notice for a while, so I'd drop a few context clues. Turn on a little music from my favorite Disney soundtrack, or put Mickey Mouse ears on my head.

But as soon as they realized where we were going, there was always a nuclear explosion of joy. That energy would last until the ride home, when they inevitably crashed in their car seats. To date, these are some of the most cherished parenting memories I share with my daughter and my son. We'd ride Pirates of the Caribbean over and over, singing "Yo ho" at the top of our lungs.

We watched every show, attended every parade, and at the end of a long, hot day…we'd grab mouse-shaped frozen pops and make our way back to the castle for the magical grand finale.

I'm not gonna lie, I'm tearing up right now just remembering those firework moments. My two little babies pressed in close, the happy, uplifting music, the explosions of color you can feel in your chest. The wonder on my babies' faces.

And then, after Tinker Bell flew from the castle, it was back to reality for everyone.

Lemme just say, reentry could be rough. That's the only Disney criticism I have. They call it the Happiest Place on Earth for a reason—and that reason sure as heck ain't the parking lot.

Still, I'll take my babies to Disney any chance I can get. I want my children to know that feeling for as long as they possibly can. Where everything's safe, and everyone's loved, and it's okay to believe you can fly.

I know it's all just a man-made fantasy. But deep down, I feel like it shouldn't be.

In this era of facing my delusions, though, I've come to see things more clearly. The reason I love Disney is not because flaws don't exist there, but because they're so well covered. Let's be real—the place would stink of body odor if there weren't scents being sprayed in every corner. I walk past Pirates of the Caribbean, and I get a whiff of sweet rum. I wander through Adventureland, and Aladdin's camel is spitting water while the air smells like citrus and orange whip. It's not real, but it's believable.

And to be honest, my relationship with church wasn't too different. I bought into the smoke-and-mirrors show of so many places, and I forgot about the underbelly. I bought into that delusion so fully that I felt like I was walking around Disney World, where everything was safe. But in my healing journey, I've realized that seeing things clearly is necessary. I can still enjoy Disney World and know there's pee on the pavement.

But what about my delusions about church?

I'm not sure there's enough perfume to get me to stomach some things. I had liked that little Methodist church on the mountain. It felt real. Would I prefer a fairy-tale land where we all held hands, agreed on theology, and sang "It's a Small World" with smiles on our faces? Sure. But at least it was a place where sick people were honest, and it didn't feel like a castle-in-the-sky lie.

But as much as I loved that little safe haven, we hadn't been going as a family too much. I think I had a little PTSD because since the beginning of my divorce, we hadn't gone much at all. Prior experience had taught me that churches weren't safe places when things weren't going well.

But recently my son, who is now ten years old, walked up to the couch as I was sitting there drinking my coffee.

"Mom," he asked, "what are we doing this weekend?"

Now, this child is a clever one. Before he asks me for something specific, he does some recon work. Tries to flush out a few of the reasons I might have to say no in the first place. If he was asking what we were doing this weekend, that could only mean one thing: that he wanted to do something, and he knew what it was, and he just hadn't told me yet.

"We don't have any plans," I said. "But I do need some rest this weekend."

I felt like that left things vague enough that I could decline without too much protest.

"Well, I was wondering if we could do something," he said.

"Something" is a pretty broad term. I figured the kid wanted to go to the beach, or a friend's house, or, heck, even Disney World. When his mind gets rolling it can go pretty far. Nothing is beyond the scope.

"What specifically do you want to do, Ben?"

"I just wanted to go to church on Sunday."

"Church?" I was plainly confused. He'd always complained about church days. "Is there some reason you're wanting to go back?"

He shrugged a ten-year-old shrug.

"I dunno, Mom; it's not that deep."

"Okay, son," I replied. "Lemme think about it."

I can't put my finger on the moment my reconstruction officially began, but I know that over the last several decades my faith journey has been quite a journey of ups and downs. Three baptisms, two years in ministry, and one unexpected divorce later, I found myself walking back into church with both of my children in tow. To be honest, I don't know what I expected to find. Or for that matter, what I was looking for. The picture of Jesus I'd held in my heart had been stripped to its egg-white walls.

John began preaching and I looked at the morning program. The sermon was coming from the book of Matthew, which saw Jesus hanging out with the Pharisees. These were the church folk of Christ's time—and they were also a political party. They knew the Law, they lived by its letter, and they were frequently trying to stump Jesus. Anytime church folk and Jesus got together, shenanigans were bound to ensue.

At this point in the story, tensions were building because Jesus had just told three parables—all of those stories were not-so-veiled jabs at each of the religious groups listening. At this point, the Pharisees were the only ones left and they were pretty much over this guy. So they hatched a plan to force Jesus into saying something that could get Him arrested. That's where John picked up the story:

> *Hearing that Jesus had silenced the Sadducees, the Pharisees got together. One of them, an expert in the law, tested him with this question: "Teacher, which is the greatest commandment in the Law?" Jesus replied: "'Love the Lord your God with all your heart and with all your soul and with all your mind.' This is the first and greatest commandment. And the second is like it: 'Love your neighbor as yourself.' All the Law and the Prophets hang on these two commandments."*
>
> (MATTHEW 22:34–40)

Now, for a little context. The Pharisees had developed a system of 613 religious laws. They were rigid about following them, and as one might imagine, this produced a very cool brand of righteousness.

Not only had Jesus, in one fell swoop, pulled the covers off all that legalism—He'd also outlined a gospel that was radically inclusive and simple.

I've been quoting that Scripture my whole entire life, but this was the first time it changed me. Jesus didn't hit "delete" on the old laws. He boiled them down to a tincture. In essence, He defined for everyone the Spirit of the Law. Upon which every law and every word of every prophet was hung.

Love God, and love your neighbor as yourself. The Spirit of the Law is love.

My entire life, I've been a Spirit-led person. In everything I do, my whole heart goes out ahead of me. It's why I connect so much with Christmas, with its spirit of giving and kindness. It's the reason I cry watching fireworks shows. The spirit of innocence and childhood. It's the reason I was moved so much by that prayer, holding hands with drag queens and strangers. Because in that moment, I was experiencing the Spirit of the gospel. I was fully connecting with love.

If the gospel of Jesus was really that simple, and I was starting to believe that it was…this was a Rabbi I wanted to follow.

And a faith worth reconstructing.

Sitting on a pew in that quiet Methodist church, as my friend was finishing his sermon, I felt my spirit stir in a way that I'd never before felt in a church. Jana took the stage to sing a hymn while John was preparing Communion. There was no fire or brimstone, no dramatic altar call, and I wasn't gonna need more water.

"Here we practice an open table…"

And that was the final nudge. I got my cracker, and my little cup of juice, and I bowed my head and prayed.

Yes, Lord. I will follow You.

But Your fan club really sucks.

· · · · · · · · · ·

I stood there in front of that egg-white wall, where my picture of Jesus once lived. In my pocket were three glass tiles. The beginning of my reconstruction. The hope of a more beautiful Jesus.

Love God. Love your neighbor. Those two tiles went straight on the wall.

It has always been simple, hasn't it?

And yet, that wasn't the complete gospel.

All this time, there was a tiny essential tile missing from the picture. It was an implication, so easy to overlook. But its absence from my whole faith picture had devastated everything.

As yourself.

Of course, I hadn't been loving myself. How could I, by the letter of the Law? I believed I was, as a sinner, separated from God, by nature an object of His wrath. He was so disgusted with who I was that He'd tortured His Son on the cross. No wonder my faith kept falling apart. I'd been saved into hating myself.

How much different would my faith have been if I believed I was intrinsically lovable? How much trauma could I have avoided, if I knew, deep in my heart, I was good?

God told me I was fearfully and wonderfully made, but that's not what the church was telling me. They patted my sweet little sinful head and said, "Sure He loves you. With a few small exceptions."

Turned out those exceptions were neither few nor small. I was sold two-thirds of a gospel.

Love God with all your heart, soul, and mind.

And love your neighbor...as yourself.

I wasn't just given permission to love; this was a whole dang directive to do it. Jesus assumed that I loved myself.

I'm a child of God, after all. Why shouldn't I?

I looked back up at the vast empty wall and imagined a shimmering Jesus. A colorful, cosmic mosaic. I don't know if the picture is gonna turn out right, or if I'm ever going to get to finish this work.

That's okay. That's why it's called faith.

Love God, love your neighbor.

As yourself, dear one.

I'm in love with the words of this Rabbi.

I hold up the beauty of that tiny little message and examine it once in the sun. This faith was more clear, more brilliant, and more sturdy than the one that had come tumbling down.

So I walk back up to that egg-white wall and lovingly place one more tile.

ACKNOWLEDGMENTS

It's crazy how, when life goes flying off the road, you find out who your people are.

To the ones who held me when I lost the wheel—this book would not exist without you.

To Mike Salisbury, my agent:
You believed in my voice from the very beginning, and I will never forget that.

Thank you for your guidance, your advocacy, and most especially for introducing me to Jeni's Ice Cream.

To Beth Adams, my editor:
You walked this book through fire—and sometimes had to drag me through it, too.

In every missed deadline, every excuse tangled in grief, you held space and grace for me.

Thank you for being a friend.

To Ben and Holland:

You are the joy I come home to.

You color these pages—and my life—with so much laughter and heart. You get the best of me and the worst of me, which means you get the most of me. And while I may not always be perfect, you can always count on my love.

To Mom:

I'll never stop being grateful for how you show up for me when I need you most.

For answering every phone call, for driving to me in the middle of the night, for loving me without pause. I love you *three times more*.

To Joe Joe:

Thanks for being the voice of reason when mine went quiet for a while. And sorry I freaked out when you ran over the squirrel. (To be fair, it was pretty disturbing.)

To Dad:

For staying with me when the road got rough and for reminding me that sometimes every path is hard—and you just have to choose your hard.

And DD, for sticking with this big crazy family in times that asked a lot of all of us.

To my siblings—Karen Leigh, Ty, Justin, and Jackson:

A built-in mafia of best friends who I can call anytime and who will ride at midnight. Your presence in my life means more than I've ever been able to say out loud. I love y'all.

To Clarebear and Stephanie:
My Buhbees. You are my constant in every season. Even when you couldn't physically be here, your presence was always felt.

And when you did show up, you lifted my heart off the ground with hiking, karaoke, and so much laughter. Y'all remind me who I am, and I love you to pieces.

To Danielle:
Thank you for your love, for the late-night texts, for the random prescriptions of prednisone, and for every hug when I was crying so hard I wasn't sure my eyes would open the next day.

You never once made me feel like I was too much. You are everything a neighbor and a friend should be.

To Matthew Stapley:
Loving you is like having a Disney princess for a best friend. Your sunshine energy, your animal sidekicks, your magic powers… You are a beautiful soul who brings so much joy to the world. Thank you for making me laugh when nothing else was funny. I'm so lucky to have you.

To Lauren:
My lifelong best friend. You've laid witness to my whole life and held all of my secrets like a vault.

You're the truest friend I've ever known. And I love you, Twigget.

To Monte Sano, my healing mountain:

For every mile, every whispered prayer, every breath I forgot to take until I stepped into your trees—thank you. You gave me space to grieve and heal. You gave me back to myself, one slow walk at a time.

And finally, to "My Good Friend" Matt:

One chapter changed the trajectory of my entire story—and that chapter began with you.

You're my best friend and the safest place I've ever known. I just know that my most beautiful stories from here on out will carry your name or your fingerprints. I love you BIG.

ABOUT THE AUTHOR

Mary Katherine Backstrom is best known for her viral videos and candid writing on family, faith, and mental health. She has been featured on the *TODAY* show and CNN, and in the *New York Times*—but her friends and family are most impressed with her onetime appearance on *Ellen*. MK resides in Alabama with her children and two stinky dogs. When she isn't writing, MK can be found in the woods, hiding from all the world's problems.